APPRENTICES OF CONNECTICUT 1637-1900

APPRENTICES OF CONNECTICUT 1637-1900

By Kathy A. Ritter

P.O. Box 476
Salt Lake City, UT 84110

Library of Congress Catalog Card Number 85-052453
ISBN Number 0-916489-14-0   (Hardbound)
ISBN Number 0-916489-19-1   (Paperback)

First Printing 1986
10 9 8 7 6 5 4 3 2 1

Printed in the United States of America

This work is dedicated to my great-great-grandfather, Ira P. Sweetland, who has made tracing his ancestry a frustrating challenge and an ultimate joy.

ACKNOWLEDGEMENTS

I wish to thank the many librarians along the way who shared with me their time, experience, and most of all their patience.

Special thanks to the staff at the Connecticut State Library for their unlimited help and remarkable tolerance and endurance.

I also wish to thank Dorenda Nolte and Linda Sweda for the proofreading, Barbara Brown for the many contributions, Terry Meyers for typing the index, and Irene Morgan and Kathy Kaye for the computer expertise.

Others deserving mention: Ruth Sweetland, Scott and Sandford Scott, Gary and B. J. Bolin, Avis and Stan Edwards, Neal and Helen Rogers, Ruth Smith, Sandford and Bobbie Scott, Dr. Thomas Geary, Joan Parenzo, Gene Knox, Paul O'Donnell, Bessie and Kenneth Ritter, Karen Thorne, and Brian Rosansky.

Photo by Ira Nosik

ABOUT THE AUTHOR

Kathy Ritter has been actively involved with genealogy for six years. She has traveled extensively throughout the northeastern United States while compiling her family history and, with the exception of some British ancestors, has found most of her roots there.

Kathy was born in Tariffville, Connecticut, and now resides in Windsor Locks. She is a member of the Connecticut Society of Genealogists and the Connecticut Historical Society. A recent liberal arts graduate of Asnuntuck College, her hobbies are genealogy, computers (programming), theatre, photography, and researching pirates. This is Kathy's first published work.

INTRODUCTION

While searching census records at the Connecticut State Library looking for my great-great-grandfather, Ira P. Sweetland, I found him listed in the 1850 census in the home of Luther Martin of Mansfield. It occurred to me that he might have been an indentured servant. As I began checking into sources available for indentureship contracts, I found that these records were scattered amongst various records. While I searched for my Sweetland ancestor, I abstracted all the indenture contracts I came across. In doing this research, I discovered many valuable indentureship contracts, each containing vital information for the genealogist.

Frequently when tracing ancestry, a genealogist can find a birth record and a marriage record of his ancestor, but the time between birth and marriage is, for the most part, unaccounted for. Since the average age of the apprentice was sixteen, apprenticeship records can provide important information to fill that gap. Many of the contracts I abstracted not only listed the birthdate and parentage of the apprentice, but also listed the names of the remarried parents and circumstances of the indenture. Some apprentices stated the town and country in which they were born. Typically, males were indentured until age twenty-one, females until age eighteen.

Apprenticeship records introduced me to some unusual surnames which were not listed in the standard reference sources in the State Library. Perhaps the apprenticeship record is the only official record of such persons.

Children were not the only people to become indentured servants. In order not to become charges to the town, adults were sometimes bound to one another to satisfy a debt or to learn how to make a living more efficiently.

One of the most fascinating areas I came upon were the runaway announcements in the newspapers. Apprentices were not always happy in their placements and, not infrequently, ran away. The master would sometimes place an ad in the local newspaper describing the apprentice, occasionally making disparaging remarks regarding his servant.

This work is not intended to be the final word on apprentices of Connecticut. It is an abstract of those indentureship papers I was able to locate at the various facilities listed in the "Sources" section at the end of the book. It consists primarily of Connecticut people but does contain references to New York, Massachusetts, Ohio, Rhode Island, Ireland, Amsterdam, England, and Cuba. There are approximately 2,700 surnames in the index and it covers a time period of 1637-1900. Most of the entries, however, are from the 1700s.

The material contained in this book was created by abstracting the original indenture document, which can be found by checking the source code in the lower right hand section of each entry and referring to the corresponding listing in the "Sources" section.

The index to this book does not relist the names of apprentices since they are arranged alphabetically in the work. It does, however, list other names given throughout the book who were either the masters or other interested parties.

The wording of the indenture paper changed through the years but a typical indenture would be similar to the following:

> During all which said term the said apprentice he/her said master and mistress honestly, and faithfully shall serve their secrets keep close their lawful and reasonable commands every where gladly do, and perform, damage to her said master and mistress he/she shall not willfully do; he/her master and mistress goods he/she shall not waste, embezzle, purloin, or lend unto others, nor suffer the same to be wasted or purloined; but with his/her power shall forthwith discover, and make known the same unto his/her master or mistress. Taverns nor ale-houses he/she shall not frequent: At cards, dice, or any other unlawful games he/she shall not play: Fornication he/she shall not commit, nor matrimony contract with any person during the said term: from his/her master and mistress services he/she shall not at any time unlawfully absent his/herself. But in all things as a good, honest, and faithful servant, and apprentice shall bear and behave him/herself towards his/her master and mistress during the full term abovesaid.

The master or mistress would be bound to do the following:

In consideration thereof, doth covenant, promise, grant and agree unto, and with their said apprentice in manner and form following that he/she will teach said apprentice or cause him/her to be taught by the best ways to read and write English and also the trade of _____ (if the said apprentice be capable to learn) and will find and provide for and unto the said apprentice good and sufficient meat, drink, washing, lodging and apparel fitting for an apprentice during the said term. At the end of the said term to dismiss the said apprentice with two suits of clothes one fit for working day and the other suitable for holy days.

If you are searching for an ancestor whom you believe was an apprentice or had apprentices and do not find him/her in this book, I suggest you search the following types of records: Justice of the Peace records, town records, court records, treasurer accounts, family records, diaries, land records andprobates. Check also, in this book and other records, for alternate spellings of surnames, e.g. Saunders (Sanders); Little (Lytle); Rawley (Rowley). Early record-keepers were frequently unconcerned with accurate spelling.

Incidentally, I never did find the indentureship contract of Ira P. Sweetland.

TRADES

Below are listed some of the trades which are found in this work with a brief definition.

Blacksmith	-	Forger of iron
Cooper	-	Barrel maker
Cordwainer	-	Shoemaker
Housewifery	-	Domestic chores
Husbandry	-	Farmer
Joiner	-	Carpenter
Roper	-	Rope maker
Shipwright	-	Ship builder
Silversmith	-	Forger of silver
Tinker	-	Works with tin
Wheelwright	-	Builds wheels
Whitesmith	-	Tinsman

To all People to whom these Presents shall come I William Bacon of Providence in the County of Providence and Colony of Rhode Island &c Truchman send Greeting. Whereas my Apprentice Asa Belles Son of Priscilla Belles of Canterbury in the County of Windham in the Colony of Connecticutt hath divers years yet to come and unexpired of his Apprenticeship, Viz, Eighteen years and Eleven Months from the Eleventh Day of May A D 1769 as by his Indenture of Apprenticeship to Me Sealed doth appear; NOW Know &c That I the said William Bacon for Divers Good Causes and Considerations Me hereto moving have given, Granted Assigned and Set over and by these Presents Do fully and absolutely Give Grant, Assign and Set over unto William Adams of Norwich in the County of New London in the Colony of Connecticutt Yeoman all Such Right Title Duty Term of Years to come, Service and Demand whatsoever which I the said William Bacon have in to the said Asa Belles which I may or ought to had in him by force and Virtue of the said Apprenticeship. And moreover I the said William Bacon do by these Presents Covenant Promise and agree to and with the said William Adams his Executors and Administrators that notwithstanding anything by Me the said William Bacon to be done to the contrary the said Asa Belles shall during the Residue of the said Term of years well and truely Serve the said William Adams as his Master and his Commandments Lawful and honest shall do, and from his Service shall not absent himself during the said Term. Provided that the said William Adams shall well intreat and use him the said Asa Belles and shall provide for him during the Residue of said Term good and Sufficient Meat Drink Cloathing Washing and Lodging as well in Sickness as in Health, and learn him to read and write and at the Expiration of the said Term to dismiss him with Two good Suits of Apparell for all parts of his Body and a good Bible as is fit and Usual for such an Apprentice

This Indenture

made the *twenty sixth* Day of *September* in the Year of our Lord One Thousand Seven hundred and Ninety *seven* BETWEEN *Benjamin Tallmadge of the Town of Litchfield & State of Connecticut of ~~the City of New York~~*, of the one Part, and *John Philip Monigati & Margaretha his* ~~Wife Passengers from Amsterdam on board the Ship Boyne, Gilbert Floyd owner~~ of the other Part, WITNESSETH, that the said *John Philip Monigati* now aged *thirty three Years, & Margaratha his Wife now aged twenty Eight Years*

in Consideration of the Covenants and Agreements herein after mentioned, on the Part of the said *Tallmadge* doth by these Presents, of *their* own free Will and Accord, put and bind *themselves* to the said *Tallmadge* to serve *him* the said *Tallmadge his* Executors, Administrators and Assigns, according to the best of *their* Power and Skill, faithfully and honestly, during the Term of *Three full Years* from the Date hereof, in all lawful Business and Matters that the said *Tallmadge* may direct; And the said *Tallmadge* for *himself his* Executors, Administrators, and Assigns, doth covenant with the said Servants that *he* will find, allow, and furnish *them* the said Servants during the Term of Service aforesaid with sufficient Meat, Drink, Washing, Lodging, and Wearing Apparel, *& also pay to the said Gilbert Floyd, or to the Owners of the Ship the Sum of One hundred & fifty seven Dollars — The food apparel & being such as shall be* fitting for a Person in *this* Station. *And the said Servants further Covenant that they will serve the said Tallmadge the additional Period of six months for each Child which shall be born to them during the aforesaid Period of their Indenture* IN WITNESS whereof the said Parties have hereunto interchangeably set their Hands and Seals, the Day and Year first above written.

Sealed and Delivered
in the Presence of

Johann Philip Monigoti

Margrethe ✝ Monigati
her
mark

Benj Tallmadge

WM Strong

Rich x Floyd

Whereas Jonathan Calkins and Samuel Calkins both of New London in the County of New London Sons of Thomas Calkins Late of New London Decd. have Represented to the Select men of s.d New London that their father and mother are both now deceased and Left them and a Young Brother Thomas Calkins that their s.d Mother was Guardian to s.d Thomas and put him Apprentice unto her Son aforsd. Samuel Calkins with whom he Lived Some time before his s.d Mother's Death, and that his s.d Mother and Guardian Intended to have bound her s.d Son Thomas to his s.d Brother Samuel, but being taken away by Death was prevented and now the s.d Thomas Refuses to Choose another Guardian and to be bound to any body, and Chooses a Loose Lazy Life, and is in Danger of being Ruined and come to Nothing and become unserviceable to himself or the Common wealth if not bound out to a Trade, and to Do business.

Therefore we James Mumford Joseph Hurlbut and Jeremiah Chapman all of New London afors.d and Select men of the Town of New London by and with the Consent and approbation of John Richards Justice of the Peace for the County of New London, Do put and bind the Said Thomas Calkins Apprentice unto Samuel Calkins of said New London Shoe Maker or Cordwainer and with him the Said Samuel Calkins to Dwell and faithfully to Serve to Learn his art or Trade of a Shoe maker until the s.d Thomas Shall Arrive to the Age of Twenty one Years During Said Term, the s.d Apprentice his Said Master faithfully Shall Serve and not absent himself from his s.d Service without Leave or Liberty but in all things Shall bear and behave himself towards his Said Master as a Good and faithfull Apprentice ought.

In Consideration whereof the s.d Samuel Calkins Promises to teach the Said Apprentice the Art, Trade or Mistery of a Shoe Maker or Cordwainer So as to be a workeman at s.d Trade if s.d Apprentice be Capable to Learn and also teach him to Read writs and Cypher to find and provide to and for s.d Apprentice Sufficient and Suitable meat, drink washing Lodging and Apparel During Said Term and the End of said Term dismiss the s.d Apprentice from his Said Service with Two Suits of Apparrell from head to foot one Suitable for Holy days, the other for Labour. In witness whereof we s.d James have hereunto Set their hands and Seals this day of January Anno Dom. 1763

Signed Sealed and Deliv.d
In presence of

J. Mumford
Jos. Hurlbut
Jer. Chapman

I John Richards do Consent to
and approve of the above
Indentures of Thomas Calkins
John Richards Jus. Pac.

This INDENTURE Witnesseth,

THAT *Christopher Fisher a poor Lad of the age of fifteen years the 13th of last September born in portsmouth in England but now Resident in new London in the County of New London and Colony of Connecticut in new England in want and distress having neither master parent nor Guardian* doth by and with the Consent of the Selectmen of said new London *and himself out unto Benjamin Henshaw of said town in the County of New London and Colony aforesaid merchant*

And with *him* the said *Benjamin Henshaw* —————— after the Manner of an Apprentice to Dwell, and Serve during the Term of *his arival to the age of Twenty one Years*

During all which said Term the said Apprentice his said M*aster* ————— Honstly, and Faithfully shall Serve, *his* Secrets keep Close, *his* lawful and reasonable Commands every where gladly Do, and Perform, Damage to *his* said M*aster* he shall not wilfully Do, *his* M*asters* Goods he shall not Waste, Embezel, Purloine, or Lend unto Others nor suffer the same to be Wasted, or Purloined; but with h*is* Power shall forthwith Discover, and make Known the same unto h*is* M*aster* Taverns, nor Ale Houses he shall not frequent: At Cards, Dice, or any other unlawful Game he shall not Play: Fornication he shall not Commit, nor Matrimony Contract with any Person during the said Term: From h*is* M*asters* Service he shall not absent any Time unlawfully Absent *himself*. But in all Things as a good, honest, and faithful Servant, and Apprentice shall Bear, and Behave *himself* towards *his* said M*aster* during the full Term aboveaid.

And the said *Benjamin Henshaw* In CONSIDERATION THEREOF, ————— Doth Covenant, Promise, Grant and Agree unto, and with *his* said Apprentice, in Manner and Form following, THAT IS TO SAY, that he will Teach h*is* said Apprentice, or cause h*im* to be Taught, by the best Ways, and Means that he may, or can, *the art and Business of a Sailor or Seaman also to Read write and Cypher together with the mariners art or art of Navagation*

(if the said Apprentice be capable to Learn) and will find and provide for and unto the said Apprentice good and sufficient *meat washing Lodging & Cloathing in Sickness and in health* —

Fitting for an Apprentice during the said Term: And at the End of the said Term to Dismiss the said Apprentice *with one good Suit of apparel Suitable for a Seaman*

IN TESTIMONY whereof, The said Parties to these present INDENTURES have Interchangeably set their Hands and Seals the *29th* ————— Day of *July* In the *11th* Year of the Reign of Our Sovereign Lord *George the third* by the Grace of God of Great-Britain, France, and Ireland, KING. Annoque Domini, One Thousand Seven Hundred and Seventy *one*

Signed, Sealed, and Delivered
in Presence of
Thos Law
Edwd Palmes

Benjamin Henshaw

Christopher Fisher

New London August ye 10th Day 1761.

To ye Select men of New London Gentlemen I have
agreed to bind My Son John Congdon to David Rogers
as an apprintice by your assistance on the following
terms (viz.) Sd Rogers is to find him Meat Drink
washing and Lodging and Cloathing suitable for an
apprintice During sd whole time of his apprintiship
and to Give him two Sutes of apparil when his
time is up, which will be ye 5th Day of march AD 1771 or he was
and he is to Learn him to Read write and

was born ye 7th Day of march AD 1750

Cipher as far as the Rule of three and he is to Learn
him ye trade of a black Smith Gentlemen the Compliance
with the above will Much oblige your friend to
Serve you

John Jenkins

Ruth Congdon

Stephen Gardner

Farmington April 16th ~ 1806

We the subscribers certify that in our opinion

the habitual complaints of Solomon Carrington are connected with effects occasioned by the amputation of his leg — — — —

Eli Todd
Fany Wadsworth

APPRENTICES

ABBE, DANIEL, of Mansfield, bound to Skiff Freeman of Mansfield until age 21, which will be 15 JUL. 1819, to learn trade of servant.

IND. DATE: 03 Jan. 1814   CSL-001

ABBOT, JAMES - Towns of Lebanon and Columbia agree to support the following people and will bind them out as said towns see fit:

James Abbot, Pricilla Pimmes, The Widow Miriam Allen, Eunice Thomas & child, Salley Brown, Prudence Curtiss, Otis Little, Ruth Forb(e)s, The Widow Elizabeth Baxter, Lucy Lyman and shall pay $10 to town of Lebanon for support of Ceazar Bissel and his wife Cloe for life.

IND. DATE: 30 Oct. 1805   COT-001

ADDAMS, BENJAMIN - Probate in Hartford District - Farmington dated 05 Sep. 1655. William Addams provides that his children are to be placed out: Benjamin age 6, Elizabeth age 3, Samuel Heacock age 12, and Joseph Heacock age 10.

RECORD DATED: 05 Sep. 1655   CSL-002

ADECON, JOHN, of S. Tolland, child of Elisabeth Crandel of S. Tolland, bound to Jonathan Ball of S. Tolland until age 21 to learn the trade of husbandry.

IND. DATE: 23 Nov. 1787   CSL-003

ALDERMAN, ELISHA, ran away from Solomon Allyn of Windsor. Elisha is age 20, 5' 8" tall, has black hair and is freckled.

NEWSPAPER DATED: 10 Jul. 1769   CTC-001

ALLEN, ANDREW, of Mansfield, bound to Horace Reed of Enfield until age 21 which will be on 10 Sep. 1851 to learn the trade of husbandry.

IND. DATE: 25 Jan. 1845   CSL-001

ALLEN, CLARISSA, bound to Joseph Loomis and wife Mary until age 18, which will be on 17 May 1794.

IND. DATE: 28 Apr. 1788   CSL-004

ALLEN, JEDEDIAH, bound to Saxton Bailey and wife Lois of Lebanon until age 21, which will be on 23 March 1800, to learn the trade of joiner.

IND. DATE: 18 May 1795   CSL-004

ALLEN, LEVI, of Suffield, bound to Josiah Coy of West Suffield until age 21, which will be on 25 Mar. 1813, to learn trade of joiner.

IND. DATE: 21 Dec. 1801   KML-001

ALLYN, THOMAS, ran away from Samuel Foot of Torrington. Thomas is age 19, tall and slim. Reward $2.

NEWSPAPER DATED: 16 Jul. 1798   CTC-001

ALLEN, WILLIAM H. JR., aged about 16 on 07 Jul. 1868, child of Wm. H. Allen, bound to Case Lockwood & Brainard Company of Hartford until age 21, which will be on 14 Sep. 1871, to learn the trade of compositor.

IND. DATE: 24 Sep. 1868   CHS-001

AMMOT, JOHN, of Wethersfield, child of Widow Mary Belden of Wethersfield, bound to Benjamin Mann of West Springfield, Massachusetts, until age 21, which will be on 15 Oct. 1800, to learn trade of blacksmith.

IND. DATE: 28 Apr. 1784   CSL-005

AMMET, JOHN, of Wethersfield, child of Widow Mary Belden of Wethersfield, bound to Jason Boardman of Wethersfield until age 21, which will be on 01 Sep. 1800, to learn trade of navigation.

IND DATE: 05 Jan. 1795   CSL-005

ANDERSON, DANIEL, of Wethersfield, child of Sawney Anderson of Glastonbury, bound to Roger Brown of Wethersfield until age 21, which will be on 02 Feb. 1785, to learn trade of cordwainer.

IND. DATE: 28 Jan. 1783   CSL-005

ANDERSON, ELSE, of Glastonbury, aged 12 March 1 last, daughter of Sonny Anderson of Glastonbury, bound to Elisha Hale of Glastonbury until age 18 to learn trade as servant.

IND. DATE: 16 Feb. 1785   CSL-006

ANDERSON, SONNY, of Glastonbury, age 17 years the 8th day instant December, child of Sonny Anderson of Glastonbury, bound to Elisha Hale of Glastonbury until age 21 to learn the trade of cooper.

IND. DATE: 22 Dec. 1789   CSL-006

ANDRUS, ASA JR., of Wethersfield, child of Asa Andrus and wife Cloe of Wethersfield. Bound to Frederick Robbins of Wethersfield until age 21, which will be on 23 Dec. 1801, to learn the trade of farming. Cloe Andrus is now Cloe Colton.

IND. DATE: 11 Apr. 1791   CSL-005

ANDRUS, ELLEN C., inmate of poor house of Farmington, child of Thomas Andrus of Farmington, bound to William B. Slade of Farmington until age 18, which will be on 22 Oct. 1866, to learn trade of housewifery.

IND. DATE: 08 Aug. 1851   CSL-007

ANDRUS, FREDERICK, of Wethersfield, child of Asa Andrus bound to Obadiah Smith of Wethersfield until age 21, which will be on 24 Jul. 1789, to learn trade of shoemaker or tanner.

IND. DATE: 26 Jan. 1784   CSL-005

ANDRUS, GEORGE RODNEY, of Farmington, child of Thomas Andrus, bound to John D. Hills of Farmington until 01 Apr. 1861, at which time he will be aged 16 years, 3 months, 25 days, to learn the trade of farming.

IND. DATE: 01 Apr. 1854   CSL-007

ANDREWS, JONATHAN - ran away from David Andrews of Glastonbury. Jonathan is age 11, and has dark hair. Reward 3 shillings.

NEWSPAPER DATED: 21 Aug. 1786   CTC-001

ARIAIL, JOHN - ran away from Theodore Cowles of New Hartford. John is age 17, 5' 7" tall, has short, brown hair and knows saddler trade. Reward $2.

NEWSPAPER DATED: 25 Jun. 1792   CTC-001

ARMSTRONG, HANNAH M. - Letter to Lebanon from Voluntown: Hannah M. Armstrong, widow of Amaziah Armstrong dec., a resident of Lebanon now in Voluntown 09 Nov. 1868, is in home of her son-in-law Cyrus Foster. The woman is 87 years old and crippled. Her daughter (unnamed) offers to keep her for $1 a week. (Lebanon denies daughter's request).

RECORD DATED: 09 Nov. 1868   LTH-001

ARNOLD, JOHN, of Hartford, bound to Ann Sandford of Hartford for term of 15 years, 3 months, at which time he will be age 21.

IND. DATE: 29 Dec. 1676   CSL-008

ARNOLD, SARAH - Bpt. 6 May 1770, a poor child bound out by the townsmen to Rev. Izrahiah Wetmore. "Sarah is supposed to be 6 years of age."

RECORD DATED: 06 May 1770   CSL-009

ATWELL, CHARLES, of New London, bound to Elihu Avery of New London until age 21 to learn the trade of shoemaker.

IND. DATE: 06 Nov. 1780   CSL-010

AVERY, GEORGE, of Bolton, aged about 7 on 19 Feb. 1848, bound to Wm. Keeney of Bolton until age 21 to learn the trade of servant.

IND. DATE: 15 May 1848   CSL-011

AVERY, MAJOR GRISWOLD - Letter signed by Collins Gorton, New London, dated 28/May/1778. Agreement to (submit) a dispute between Amos Beebe and Truman Crocker - wherein Beebe challenges said Crocker of having not fulfilled his covenant in said indenture to Major Griswold Avery.

RECORD DATED: 28 May 1778   CSL-010

AYRES, JOHN C., bound to Robert Douglas of Waterford until age 21.

IND. DATE: 17 Sep. 1832   WTH-001

AYERS, ROBERT, of New London, bound to Alexander Pygan Adams of New London for a term of 5 years, 6 months, 24 days, until age 21 to learn the trade of seaman/navigation.

IND. DATE: 06 Apr. 1772   CSL-010

AYERS, ROBERT, of New London, bound to William Cowell of Boston, Massachusetts for a term of 2 years, 9 months, 6 days, until age 21, to learn the trade of navigation.

IND. DATE: 24 Jan. 1775   CSL-010

BAB, WILLIAM, of Middletown, aged about 11, child of Benjamin Bab dec. of Middletown, bound to William Cone of Middletown until age 21, which will be on 04 Nov. 1781, to learn the trade of shoemaker.

IND. DATE: 04 Sep. 1780   MHS-001

BACCUSS, JOEL W., of Bolton, child of Abner Backus of Bolton, bound to Elijah Warner of Bolton until age 16, which will be on 09 Aug. 1839, to learn the trade of farming.

IND. DATE: 07 Sep. 1832   CSL-011

BACKUS, LYMAN, of Bolton, aged about 9 on 26 Feb. 183(6), bound to William Keney of Bolton until age 21 to learn trade of servant.

IND. DATE: 04 Jan. 1836   CSL-011

BADGER, JAMES, of Middletown, was found in schoolhouse at Longhill. Parents are unknown. He was bound to Jacob Hall of Middletown until age 16, which will be on 13 Nov. 1791, to learn trade of servant.

IND. DATE: 04 Feb. 1782   MHS-001

BAILEY, ELISHA, of Middletown, bound to Franklin Kellsey of Middletown until age 21, which will be on 12 Sep. 1846, to learn the trade of line and lace making.

IND. DATE: 04 Sep. 1843   MHS-001

BAILEY, EMMA, of Middletown, child of Noah Bailey of Middletown, bound to Thomas C. Simpson of Middletown until age 18, which will be on 09 Nov. 1861, to learn the trade of housewifery.

IND. DATE: 28 Sep. 1846   MHS-001

BAKER, ALBERT C., of Hartford, born 16 Jan. 1860, now age 20, child of Richard A. Baker, bound to Case Lockwood & Brainard Company of Hartford for a term of 2 years, to learn the trade of job pressman.

IND. DATE: 13 Dec. 1880   CHS-001

BAKER, JOHN GILBERT, of Tolland, bound to Benjamin D. Benton of Tolland until age 21 to learn the trade of farming.

IND. DATE: 01 Apr. 1837   CSL-003

BAKER, RUTH of Groton, bound to Jonathan Randall to learn the trade of housewifery.

IND. DATE: 13 Jun. 1774   ICR-004

BAKER, SAMUEL, of Glastonbury, bound to Samuel Stratton of S. Glastonbury until age 21, which will be on 15 Dec. 1795, to learn the trade of blacksmith.

IND. DATE: 09 Mar. 1784   CSL-006

BALDWIN, SAMUEL, of Milford, child of Widow Mary Baldwin of Milford, bound to James Baldwin of Milford for term of 2 1/2 years to learn trade of weaver.

IND. DATE: 01 Mar. 1698/9   CSL-020M

BANCROFT, NATHANIEL, of E. Windsor, with the consent of his guardian Samuel Allen Jr. of E. Windsor, binds himself to John Dewey Jr. of Suffield until age 21, which will be on 28 Oct. 1804, to learn the trade of joining and chairmaking.

IND. DATE: 21 Aug. 1798   KML-001

BARBER, JOSIAS, bound to Deacon John Moore until age 21.

IND. DATE: 04 Feb. 1662   CSL-012-A

BARBER, MERCY, bound to Lt. Walter Filer until age 18 - "unless she marry before with her masters and dames and eldest brothers approbation."

IND. DATE: 04 Feb. 1662   CSL-012-A

BARBER, SAMUEL, bound to "his brother Thomas" until age 21.

IND. DATE: 04 Feb. 1662   CSL-012-A

BARBER, THOMAS - Order of court that Frances Stiles is to teach his servants, George Chapple, Thomas Cooper, and Thomas Barber in the trade of carpenter.

IND. DATE: 28 Mar. 1637   CSL-012-C

BARKER, NELSON, of Harwinton, child of Ephraim Barker of Harwinton, bound to W.S. & I.G. Wetmore of Winsted until age 21, which will be on 13 Jun. 1845, to learn the trade of joiner and painter.

IND. DATE: 01 Apr. 1840   CSL-013M

BARNS, ELIZA, of Middletown, child of Sally (Marg) of Middletown, bound to William Johnson of South Farm Middletown, until age 18, which will be on 12 Aug. 1828, to learn trade of weaving.

IND. DATE: 13 Mar. 1820   MHS-001

BARNES, JAMES, of Farmington, child of Hartwell Barnes of Farmington, bound to Samuel Gridley of New Hartford until age 14, which will be on 17 Apr. 1808, to learn the trade of husbandry.

IND. DATE: 04 Dec. 1804   CSL-007

BARNES, SAMUEL, of Farmington, bound to Seth Lewis of Farmington until age 21, which will be on 20 Feb. 1841, to learn the trade of farming.

IND. DATE: 30 Sep. 1828   CSL-007

BARNS, SOPHRONIA, of Farmington, bound to Seth Lewis of Farmington until age 18, which will be on 06 Oct. 1834, to learn the trade of housewifery.

IND. DATE: 01 Oct. 1828   CSL-007

BARRET, JOSHUA, of Thompson Parish Killingly, child of Oliver Barret, bound to William Allton of Thompson Parish Killingly for term of 8 years, 3 months, and 20 days to learn the trade of husbandry.

IND. DATE: 01 Jan. 1754   STL-001

BARTHOLOMEW, JESSE, ran away from Hiram Whitcomb. Jesse has long black hair, 5' 8" tall. Reward one penny.

NEWSPAPER DATED: 31 Dec. 1792   CTC-001

BASSET, ELIAS, ran away from Ezekiel Cowles Jr. of Farmington. Height 5' 3". Reward eight milles.

NEWSPAPER DATED: 17 Jun. 1779   CTC-001

BATES, MARY, of Farmington, child of Moses Bates of Farmington, bound to Wills Alderman of Simsbury until age 18, which will be on 14 Jan. 1823, to learn the trade of housewifery.

IND. DATE: 25 Aug. 1813   CSL-007

BATH, MARY M. (Mrs.) - Appointed guardian by probate court for District of Andover to Ferdinand Warren King a ward of Columbia 14 years old.

RECORD DATED: 29 Sep. 1900   COT-003

BAXTER, DAVID, ran away from Joseph Bewell of Glastonbury. David is age 19, 5' 8" tall, short hair and light complextion. Reward 6 pence.

NEWSPAPER DATED: 20 Mar. 1781   CTC-001

BAXTER, REBECCAH, of Middletown, aged 7 years, 7 months 24 days, child of so called Hannah Barstow of Middletown, bound to Elijah Treadway of Middletown until age 18, which will be on 11 Nov. 1789, to learn the trade of tailor or housewifery. At present, Rebeccah belongs to family of her mother.

IND. DATE: 01 Jul. 1779   MHS-001

BEAL, HANNAH, of Glastonbury, bound to John Welles of Hebron until age 18, which will be on 17 Aug. 1798, to learn the trade of housewifery.

IND. DATE: 21 Dec. 1789   GHS-001

BEAL, NANCY, of Glastonbury, bound to Jehiel Bulkley and wife Mary of Wethersfield until age 18, which will be on 18 Jul. 1801, to learn the trade of spinning.

IND. DATE: 24 Mar. 1789   CSL-006

BECKWITH, ABBY, bound to William Champion.

IND. DATE: 12 Mar. 1832   WTH-001

BECKWITH, DYER, Walter Beckwith and Prince Higgins ran away from Jared Wilson Spencer, Francis Beckwith, and Oliver Warner of East Haddam. Dyer is age 19, has long, black hair and knows blacksmiths trade. Walter is 17 and knows carpenter trade and Prince is 17 and knows blacksmith trade.

NEWSPAPER DATED: 05 Aug. 1783   CTC-001

BECKWITH, GEORGE, of Lebanon, bound to Henry Otis of Lebanon until age 21, which will be on 07 Dec. 1853, to learn habits of obedience, industry, and subordination.

IND. DATE: 27 Nov. 1837   CSL-014

BECKWITH, JAMES, bound to William Moore 4th of Waterford.

IND. DATE: 31 May 1824   WTH-001

BECKWITH, LYDIA, bound to Silas Daniels.

IND. DATE: 27 Sep. 1824   WTH-001

BECKWITH, MARY ANN, bound to John A. Latimer.

IND. DATE: 21 Mar. 1825   WTH-001

BECKWITH, ROBERT, son of Lydia Beckwith, bound to Joseph Edwards.

IND. DATE: 21 Mar. 1825   WTH-001

BECKWITH, ROBERT, bound to Alfred Loomis until age 21.

IND. DATE: 20 Mar. 1826   WTH-001

BECKWITH, WILLIAM, bound to Nehemiah Caulkins.

IND. DATE: 07 Sep. 1826   WTH-001

BECKWITH, WILLIAM, bound to David G. Otis of Waterford.

IND. DATE: 04 Mar. 1829   WTH-001

BECKWITH, WILLIAM DAYTON, bound to Charles Richards.

IND. DATE: 24 Sep. 1830   WTH-001

BEEBE, ABIATHA(N), of New London. - Letter from Wm. Hillhouse to Selectmen of New London.

"Mr. Durkee bearer of note...respecting his apprentice Abiatha(n) Beebe...who has the summer past been in the service and is enlisted again for next year...the Master ye Mother and the apprentice agreed to cancel indenture.

LETTER DATED: 11 Dec. 1775   CSL-010

BEEBE, ANGELINE, of Waterford, bound to Jeremiah Chappel of Waterford.

IND. DATE: 19 Nov. 1831   WTH-001

BEEBE, ANNA, bound to Griswold Avery, Jr.

IND. DATE: 05 Sep. 1803   WTH-001

BEEBE, DAVID, of New London, bound to John Richards of Norwich until age 21 to learn the trade of card making.

IND. DATE: 22 Oct. 1782   CSL-015M

BEEBE, ELIZABETH, of New London, aged about 7, bound to Eldad Sabin and wife Abigail of Lebanon until age 18 to learn the trade of housewifery.

IND. DATE: 03 Jul. 1780   CSL-010

BEEBE, JABEZ, of New London, bound to Jacob Hox of Norwich for 16 years, 1 month, 11 days, until age 21, to learn the trade of house joiner.

IND. DATE: 04 Jun. 1770   CSL-010

BEEBE, JOSEPH, of New London, child of Stephen Beebe the 2nd dec. and wife Elizabeth of New London, bound to John Scofield of New London for term of 2 years, 2 months, 20 days.

IND. DATE: 07 Apr. 1761   CSL-010

BEEBE, JOSHUA, of New London, bound to William Fielding of New London until age 21 to learn the trade of seamanship.

IND. DATE: 01 Mar. 1779   CSL-010

BEBEE, RUPEL, of New London, aged about 13 the 20th next Aug., bound to Willard Hubbard of West London until age 21 to learn the trade of husbandry.

IND. DATE: 06 Jun. 1768   CSL-010

BEEBE, RUSSELL, of New London, age 19 the 20th instant, bound to Mary Billings of Norwich until age 21, which will be on 20 Aug. 1776, to learn the trade of husbandry.

IND. DATE: 02 Aug. 1774   CSL-010

BEEBE, SAMUEL - Selectmen of the town of Hartland warned Samuel Beebe to leave town with his family.

RECORD DATED: 06 Jul. 1762   HTH-001

BEEBE, THADDEUS, by request of his grandfather, Mr. Stephen Maynard, bound to Charles Hill of Montville.

IND. DATE: 03 May 1813   WTH-001

BEERS, JOHN FORSYTHE, bound to Asa Newton, Jr.

IND. DATE: 03 Feb. 1813   WTH-001

BELCHER, LUCRETIA, of Middletown, child of Mary Thomas of Middletown, bound to John Higbee and wife Sarah of Middletown until age 18 to learn trade of housewifery.

IND DATE: 05 May 1772   MHS-001

BELDEN, JOSIAH, of Middletown, child of Lois Phelps, bound to Samuel Baldwin, Jr. of Meriden, until age 21, which will be on 15 Apr. 1827, to learn the trade of carpenter.

IND. DATE: 02 May 1825   MHS-001

BELDEN, JOSIAH, of Middletown, child of Lois Phelps, bound to Samuel Baldwin, Jr. of Meriden, until age 21, which will be on 15 Apr. 1827, to learn the trade of carpenter.

IND. DATE: 15 Apr. 1827   MHS-001

BELL, CLARENCE E., of East Hartford, born 15Feb.1859, child of Harriet Bell, bound to Case Lockwood & Brainard Company of Hartford until age 21 to learn the trade of job pressman.

IND. DATE: 08 Feb. 1876   CHS-001

BEMENT, SAMUEL, of Middletown, child of Samuel Bement dec., with the consent of his guardian, Bezaleel Fisk, bound to George Starr of Middletown for term of 5 years to learn the trade of rope maker.

IND. DATE: 23 Jan. 1793   MHS-001

BENBREE, GERVIS - John Witchfield stated that Benbree refused to serve him the full term of his indenture.

IND. DATE: 01 Sep. 1659   CSL-012-B

BENJAMIN, CALEB, ran away from Calvin Gilman of East Hartford. Caleb is 14 years old, has black hair, small scar on chin, middling stature and dark complextion. Reward 6 pence.

NEWSPAPER DATED: 23 Jul. 1792   CTC-001

BENJAMIN, JAMES, ran away from Roswell Stanley of Hartford. James is age 16, has black hair, black eyes, stout build and knows shoemaker trade. Reward $5.

NEWSPAPER DATED: 15 Jun. 1795   CTC-001

BENNETT, EMMA PICKERING - Emma was born in Boston 01 Oct. 1863.

Emma Bennett is a child of George Augustine Bennett dec. late of Boston, Massachusetts, and Fannie Maria Bennett. Fannie is in bad health and is poor and unable to support daughter. Agreement of adoption of Emma by Edwin and Mary Alvina Reynold(s) of Mansfield.

IND. DATE: 01 Aug. 1868   CSL-001

BENNETT, GEORGE A., of Bolton, bound to Harris Hutchins of Bolton until age 17 to learn the trade of servant.

IND. DATE: 20 Jan. 1825   CSL-011

BENTON, EZEKIEL, ran away from John Ensign of Canaan. Ezekiel is age 19, 5' 10" tall, by trade a clothier.

NEWSPAPER DATED: 20 Aug. 1787   CTC-001

BENTON, MARY, of Wethersfield, bound to Daniel Wolcott of Wethersfield until age 18, which will be on 15 Jun. 1822, to learn the trade of housewifery.

IND. DATE: ( ) Nov. 1811   CSL-005

BENTON, ROYAL, of Wethersfield, bound to Joseph Tallcott of Wethersfield until age 21, which will be on 20 Mar. 1821, to learn the trade of husbandry.

IND. DATE: 14 Feb. 1816   CSL-005

BENTON, WARREN, of Tolland, child of Samuel Benton dec., bound to Orrin Benton of Tolland until age 21, which will be on 07 Mar. 1822, to learn the trade of farming.

IND. DATE: 22 Apr. 1817   CSL-003

BERRY, PEVUS, of Glastonbury, bound to Elizur Tyron of Glastonbury, until age 21, which will be on 25 Apr. 1825, to learn the trade of farming.

IND. DATE: 02 Mar. 1813   GHS-001

BETTES, ASA, child of Priscilla Bettes, bound to William Bacon.

IND. DATE: 01 May 1769   CTH-001

BETTES, ASA, child of Priscilla Bettes - Letter dated 14 Dec. 1774 - William Bacon conveys his indenture of Asa Bettes, term originally being 18 years, 11 months from 11 May 1769, to William Adams of Norwich - all rights in indenture conveyed.

RECORD DATE: 14 Dec. 1774   CSL-016M

BICKNELL, HORACE, of Mansfield, bound to Horace Bicknell of Willington until age 21, which will be on 11 Dec. 1852, to learn trade of agriculture.

IND. DATE: 13 Aug. 1832   CSL-001

BILLINGS, JABEZ, of Stonington, bound to Jedidiah Benjamin of Canterbury for 4 months to satisfy debt.

IND. DATE: 13 Apr. 1758   CHS-003

BINGAM, JOHN, child of Mary Crimmen bound to John E. Waldo.

IND. DATE: 01 Jul. 1784   CTH-001

BINGHAM, THOMAS, of Norwich, child of Thomas Bingham, bound to Ebenezer Lothrup of Norwich until age 21 to learn trade of blacksmith.

IND. DATE: 29 Oct. 1745   CSL-017M

BIRD, ISRAEL, born in England, about 30 to 40 years of age, ran away from Abraham Pettibone of Farmington. Israel is 5' 10" tall, has short, black hair, small, blue eyes, rounded shoulders, very pitted from small pox, middling body, and small limbs.

NEWSPAPER DATED: 09 Jan. 1769   CTC-001

BIRD, NATHANIEL, of Farmington, child of Joseph Bird, who died 1696, bound to Samuel Newell of Farmington until age 21 to learn the trade of carpenter or timber work.

IND. DATE: 10 Jul. 1686   FTH-001

BISSEL, HANNAH, ran away from Stephen Dormant of Granville, Massachusetts. Hannah is age 15 and has natural complextion. Reward 2 cents.

NEWSPAPER DATED: 09 May 1796   CTC-001

BLAQUE, DAVID, ran away from Thomas Brockway of Lebanon. David is age 19, large, strong build and light complextion. Reward 1 shilling.

NEWSPAPER DATED: 24 Mar. 1788   CTC-001

BLAKE, JONATHAN, of Middletown, age 16, bound to John Rogers of Middletown until age 21 to learn trade of cooper.

IND. DATE: 19 Apr. 1790   MHS-001

BLAKSLEE, OBED, of New Haven, child of Jesse Blakslee of New Haven, bound to Enos Todd of New Haven to learn the trade of shoemaker.

IND. DATE: 01 Apr. 1763   CSL-018M

BLANCHARD, JAMES, ran away from Silas Chapman of Hartford. James is short, thick set, thick dark complextion, aged 13. Took with him 3 month old black dog. Reward 3 shillings 6 pence. Return of dog only, reward 3 shillings.

NEWSPAPER DATED: 12 Sep. 1791   CTC-001

BLANCHER, WILLIAM, of Hartford, aged 3 years, 7 months, child of William Blancher late of Hartford, bound to John Easton of Hartford until age 21.

IND. DATE: 15 Apr. 1696   CSL-008

BLIN, ALMIRA, of Wethersfield, bound to Esther Williams of Middletown until age 18, which will be on 13 Jun. 1820.

IND. DATE: 13 Aug. 1814   CSL-005

BLIN, DAVID, of Wethersfield, child of Widow Hannah Blin of Wethersfield, bound to William Blin of Wethersfield until age 21, which will be on 09 May 1790, to learn trade of joiner.

IND. DATE: 02 Aug. 1784   CSL-005

BLIN, DAVID, of Wethersfield, child of Widow Hannah Blin of Wethersfield, bound to Benjamin Adams of Wethersfield until age 21, which will be on 09 May 1790, to learn trade of joiner.

IND. DATE: 12 Dec. 1788   CSL-005

BLIN, MINERVEY, of Wethersfield, bound to Mary Day of East Windsor until age 18, which will be on 08 Jun. 1824, to learn the trade of housewifery.

IND. DATE: 08 Jun. 1815   CSL-005

BOARDMAN, JOHN, ran away from Joseph Winship of Hartford. John is 5' 9" tall and is trained as mason. Reward 13 pence.

NEWSPAPER DATED: 15 Jun. 1773   CTC-001

BOLIN, GARY, son of Alton Bolin and Avis Rogers, of Simsbury was bound to B. Keirstad of Simsbury for life to learn the trade of clock maker.

IND. DATE: 10 May 1896   APR-001

BOLLES, LUCINDA, bound to Mercy Harding until age 18.

IND. DATE: 15 Sep. 1818   WTH-001

BOLTON, AMO(N), of New London, bound to Pearly Brown of Preston until age 21, which will be on 14 Oct. 1791, to learn the trade of husbandry.

IND. DATE: 11 Oct. 1782   CSL-010

BOND, BETHUEL, bound to William Carew.

IND. DATE: 13 Feb. 1775   CTH-001

BONELL, MANUEL, of Baracoa, child of Quirico Bonell, bound to Capt. Wolcott Hinsdale of Harwinton for term of 4 months (on trial) to learn trade of servant. Hinsdale agrees to take boy to New York and have him attend school.

IND. DATE: 24 Jun. 1844   LHS-001

BOOTH, SARAH, of Farmington, child of Amos Booth, bound to Edbert Cowles of Farmington until age 18, which will be in January 1829, to learn trade of servant. (indenture unfinished).

IND. DATE: 10 Aug. 1824   CSL-007

BORDO, LOUIS - Louis Bordo and wife Louisa Bordo bound themselves to town of Columbia in the sum of fifty dollars to be paid in monthly installments...said payments to come from the wages of Louis Bordo their minor child in the employ of Excelsior Web & Tape Company. of Hop River, Connecticut, Johanna Shea of Columbia pregnant with child of minor Louis Bordo agrees to release Louis from all actions.

RECORD DATED: 21 Dec. 1897   COT-002

BORKWELL, GALE G., of Middletown, bound to Asa Taylor of Suffield until 16 May 1789 to learn the trade of husbandry.

IND. DATE: 20 Aug. 1784   MHS-001

BOSTWICK, DANIEL, ran away from Amijah Jones of Salisbury. Daniel is age 15, 4' 9" tall, has yellow hair and light complextion. Reward six pence.

NEWSPAPER DATED: 10 Mar. 1778   CTC-001

BRADLEY, WILLIAM, ran away from Ebenezar Allen of Watertown. William is age 15, has red hair and freckles. Reward $2.

NEWSPAPER DATED: 21 May 1792   CTC-001

BRADY, JOHN of Hartford, born 22 Feb. 1866, child of Patrick Brady, bound to Case Lockwood & Brainard Company of Hartford until age 21, term of 3 years, 6 months, to learn trade of bookbinder.

IND. DATE: 10 Aug. 1883   CHS-001

BRAER, LAUD (Widow of), bound to John Tolery of Tolland. Tolery agrees to support Widow of Laud Braer.

IND. DATE: 13 Dec. 1831   CSL-003

BRAGG, EBENEZER, of Ashford, bound to William Johnson of Willington for 2 years to satisfy debt.

IND. DATE: 19 Jul. 1754   CHS-003

BRAMNHALL, GEORGE, ran away from Thomas Stedman, Jr. of Windham. George is age 16. Reward $4.

NEWSPAPER DATED: 20 Mar. 1769   CTC-001

BRANFORD, ISAAC, child of Isaac Branford dec. of Bolton, bound to Benjamin Talcott, Jr. of until age 16, which will be on 14 Jul. 1808, to learn the trade of servant.

IND. DATE: 09 Apr. 1804   CSL-011

BRIDGHAM, GEORGE, of Middletown, child of George Bridgham dec. bound to Elihu Stowe of Middletown, until age 21 to learn the trade of husbandry.

IND. DATE: 12 May 1794   MHS-001

BRIDGUM, SAMUEL, of Middletown, child of George Bridgum dec., bound to Jehoshaphat Starr of Middletown until age 21, which will be on 01 Jun. 1808, to learn the trade of paper making.

IND. DATE: 03 Mar. 1800   MHS-001

BRIGHT, AMELIA, aged 14 years, 6 months, 8 days, bound to Sylvester Lusk of Enfield for a term of 3 years, 5 months, 22 days, to learn the trade of housewifery. Indenture made with the consent of the Managers of Society for the Reformation of Juvenile Delinquents of New York.

IND. DATE: 13 Apr. 1832   CHS-004

BROOKS, ALBERT, bound to John Keeney until age 21.

IND. DATE: 20 Mar. 1826   WTH-001

BROOKS, CHARLES K., bound to Case Lockwood & Brainard Company of Hartford until age 21, which will be on 16 May 1871, to learn the trade of compositor. by Mrs. F. G. Bartholomew, Vice President of Hartford Orphan Asylum.

IND. DATE: 27 Jan. 1868   CHS-001

BROOKS, JOSEPH, of Wethersfield, child of Hannah Brooks, bound to Timothy Brooks of Fishkill, New York, until age 21, which will be on 16 Mar. 1788, to learn the trade of cooper.

IND. DATE: 11 Mar. 1783   CSL-005

BROOKS, MAHITABLE, of Glastonbury, bound to Elijah Welles of Glastonbury to learn the trade of housewifery.

IND. DATE: 13 Jun. 1794   GHS-001

BROTON, WILLIAM, ran away from David Richardson of Coventry. William is age 18, dark hair, light eyes, ruddy complextion, stout fellow.

NEWSPAPER DATED: 01 Jul. 1765   CTC-001

BROWN, ABNER, of New London, child of Abner Brown Jn. dec., bound to John Allen of New London until age 21 to learn trade of husbandry.

IND. DATE: 06 Sep. 1762   CSL-010

BROWN, ABNER, of New London, bound to James Shearman for term of 9 years, 2 months, 5 days, until age 21, to learn the trade of husbandman.

IND. DATE: 05 May 1772   CSL-010

BROWN, ALFRED, orphan, of Mansfield, bound to Darius Caulkins of Mansfield, until age 18, which will be on 18 Oct. 1849, to learn the trade of husbandry.

IND. DATE: 13 Jun. 1839   CSL-001

BROWN, ALVA, of Ashford, whose parents are dead, bound to Joshua Preston of Willington until age 20 to learn the trade of tanning/currying.

IND. DATE: 27 Mar. 1837   CSL-019M

BROWN, EDWARD, of Middletown, child of Mrs. Solomon, bound to Nicholas Darrow of Middletown for term of 4 years to learn the trade of husbandry.

IND. DATE: 09 Feb. 1795   MHS-001

BROWN, FRANCES ANN, child of Stephen Brown, bound to Peleg G. Thomas of Lebanon.

IND. DATE: 1839/40   CSL-004

BROWN, HARRIET, of Lebanon, child of Stephen Brown, bound to Enoch McCall of Lebanon until age 18, which will be on 08 Nov. 1844, to learn the trade of housewifery.

IND. DATE: 07 Sep. 1838   CSL-014

BROWN, JOHN M., of Lebanon, child of Stephen Brown, bound to Elias L. Williams of Lebanon until age 21, which will be on 21 Nov. 1851.

IND. DATE: 07 Sep. 1838   CSL-004

BROWN, LUCY, of Mansfield bound to Nathaniel Brown of Mansfield until age 18, which will be on 09 Oct. 1832, to learn the trade of housewifery.

IND. DATE: 06 May 1822   CSL-001

BROWN, WILLIAM E., of Lebanon, bound to Caleb F. Chappell of Montville until age 17.

IND. DATE: 19 Sep. 1857   CSL-014

BRUNNOCK, JOHN, of Groton, bound to Mortimore Stoddard of Groton until age 21.

IND. DATE: 04 Sep. 1773   ICR-002

BRUNSON, LYDIA, of Bolton, child of Isaac Brunson late of Bolton, bound to Samuel Walbridge of Coventry until age 18 to learn trade of servant.

IND. DATE: 27 Jan. 1806   CSL-011

BUCK, MIRON, of Sherman, aged about 11, child of Chloe, bound to Benjamin Akin until age 21, which will be in 10 years, to learn the trade of farming. (Miron was bound by William Duncan husband to Chloe)

IND. DATE: 07 Oct. 1822   CSL-044M

BURGE, MARY ANN - Abijah Root contracted to keep Mary Ann Burge for 3 years from 20 Dec. 1813; to be paid $25. Marked "paid in full" 03 Feb. 1817.

IND. DATE: 20 Dec. 1813   HBT-002

BULKLEY, SOLOMON, of Wethersfield, child of Mary Russell, bound to Jonathan Hand of Wethersfield, until age 21, which will be on 29 Mar. 1791, to learn trade of shoemaker.

IND. DATE: 07 Dec. 1784   CSL-005

BURIT, ISRAEL, of Stratford. Burit was arrested for running away from his master, John Glover and wife Widow Sarah. Burit's guardians claim Burit never legally bound to Glover. Jury find for Burit.

RECORD DATED: 14 Feb. 1703   CSL-GA-01

BURNHAM, CHAUNCEY, ran away from William Warner of Hartford. Chauncey is age 18, 5' 10" tall, red hair, light blue eyes, flat nose and has sandy complextion. Reward $20.

NEWSPAPER DATED: 23 Jan. 1797   CTC-001

BURNHAM, HARIOT, of Middletown, bound to Joshua Stow of Middletown until age 18 to learn the trade of housewifery.

IND. DATE: 06 Mar. 1815   MHS-001

BURNS, ENOCH, of Middletown, child of Reuben Burns, bound to Townsend Way of Middletown until age 21, which will be on 14 Mar. 1840 to learn the trade of paper staining.

IND. DATE: 03 Jun. 1835   MHS-001

BURNS, THOMAS, of Coventry, bound to Noah Porter of Coventry until age 21, which will be in June, 1824, to learn the trade of husbandry.

IND. DATE: 03 Jan. 1820   CSL-021

BURNS, THOMAS J., of Hartford, born 22 Nov. 1858, child of Thomas Burns, bound to Case Lockwood & Brainard Company of Hartford, for term of 2 years, until age 21, to learn the trade of job pressman.

IND. DATE: 22 Nov. 1877   CHS-001

BURR, CHAUNCEY, of Farmington, aged about 6 on 23 Jan. next, child of Salmon Burr, bound to Jonathan Barns of Farmington until age 15.

IND. DATE: 16 Sep. 1799   CSL-007

BURR, CHANCEY SALMON, of Farmington, child of Salomon Burr dec., bound to Noadiah Woodruff of Farmington until age 15, which will be on 23 Jan. 1809.

IND. DATE: 17 Apr. 1804   CSL-007

BURR, HEAMAN of Farmington, child of Salmon Burr, bound to Gabrail Curtiss of Farmington until age 16, which will be on 15 Sep. 1805.

IND. DATE: 10 May 1802   CSL-007

BURR, JASON, child of Salomon Burr dec. of Farmington, bound to Thomas Gridley of Bristol until age 21, which will be in January 1821, to learn the trade of husbandry.

IND. DATE: 18 Oct. 1803   CSL-007

BURR, JOSEPH, ran away from Douglas & Ely of Danbury. Joseph is 18, small for age, has dark eyes, dark complextion and is bold and assuming. Reward $10.

NEWSPAPER DATED: 14 Jan. 1793   CTC-001

BURRELL, ABIGAIL, of New London, bound to Charles Joffrey to learn trade of housewifery. (term of 12 years crossed out on indenture paper).

IND. DATE: 06 Dec. 1762   CSL-010

BUTLER, ALEXANDER, of Middletown, child of Daniel Butler dec., bound to Jacob Sawyer of Middletown, until age 21, which will be on 06 Jun. 1827, to learn trade of shoemaker.

IND. DATE: 02 Jun. 1823   MHS-001

BUTLER, DANIEL, of Middletown, child of Daniel Butler dec., bound to Frederick Bulkley of Wethersfield until age 21, which will be on 01 Sep. 1826, to learn the trade of blacksmith.

IND. DATE: 06 Nov. 1820   MHS-001

BUTLER, ISAAC, of Middletown, child of Mary the wife of Edward Reding of Middletown, bound to Samuel Ward of Middletown until age 21 to learn the trade of husbandry.

IND. DATE: 12 Apr. 1790   MHS-001

BUTRICK, EPHRAIM, and Josiah Hurlbort ran away from Elijah Porter and Peter Curtiss of Farmington. Ephraim is 19, middling stature and serving trade of foot wheels. Josiah is 19, has black hair and darkish complextion, thick set, and serving trade of blacksmith.

NEWSPAPER DATED: 29 Mar 1769   CTC-001

BUTTEN, BENJAMIN of New London, bound to Lebbeus Tubbs of New London for term of 3 years, until age 21, to learn trade of husbandry.

IND. DATE: 24 Aug. 1773   CSL-010

BUTTS, ESTHER bound to William Moore 4th Esq.

IND. DATE: 13 Jul. 1814   WTH-001

BYINGTON, BETSY, of Farmington, illegitimate daughter of the wife of Aaron Woodruff of Farmington, bound to Timothy Mix of Bristol until age 18, which will be on 28 Jun. 1801 to learn the trade of housewifery. (Indenture states that Betsy Byington was born previous to mother's marriage to Aaron Woodruff.)

IND. DATE: 03 May 1797   CSL-007

BYINGTON, BETSY, of Farmington, illegitimate daughter of the wife of Aaron Woodruff of Farmington, bound to Jesse Wilcox of Farmington until age 18, which will be on 28 Jun. 1801, to learn the trade of housewifery.

IND. DATE: 28 Apr. 1800   CSL-007

CADWELL, JOHN, of Middletown, child of John Cadwell dec., bound to Stephen Ranney of Middletown until age 21, which will be on 24 Dec. 1801, to learn the trade of boat building.

IND. DATE: 13 May 1793   MHS-001

CADY, ELIZABETH, of Pomfret, bound to William Walton of Pomfret until 29 Apr. 1777 to learn the trade of housewifery.

IND. DATE: 03 Oct. 1766   CSL-030M

CADY, TOMASON, of Pomfret bound to Israel Putnam of Pomfret until 30 Jun. 1770.

IND. DATE: 28 Aug. 1765   CSL-030M

CALAIS, JOHN of Wethersfield, child of John Calais and wife Betty, bound to Absalom Williams of Wethersfield until age 21, which will be in 1781, to learn the trade of farming.

IND. DATE: 10 Jan. 1763   CSL-005

CALKINS, FREDERICK of New London, with the approval of his guardian Stephen Prentiss of New London, bound to Simpson Carow of New London until age 21, which will be on 25 Jan. 1770, to learn the trade of mariner.

IND. DATE: 25 Apr. 1763   CSL-010

CALKINS, THOMAS, of New London, bound to Samuel Calkins of New London until age 21 to learn the trade of cordwainer. Jonathan and Samuel Calkins state parents are dead and their brother Thomas is in danger of being ruined and therefore bind him to Samuel Calkins.

IND. DATE: 07 Jan. 1763   CSL-010

CALKINS, WILLIAM, ran away from Eleazer Pomeroy of Coventry. William is age 17. Reward 6 pence.

NEWSPAPER DATED: 16 Jul. 1787   CTC-001

CALLAM, DANIEL M., of New London, age about 13, bound to James Culver of New London until age 21 to learn the trade of shoemaker and tanner.

IND. DATE: 01 Mar. 1779   CSL-010

CANNADA, BILLY, of Glastonbury, aged 16 the 13th December last, child of David Cannada, bound to James McLean of Glastonbury until age 21 to learn the trade of cooper.

IND. DATE: 13 Apr. 1790   CSL-006

CANNON, JEREMIAH, of New London, age 13, bound to William Moor of New London until age 21 to learn the trade of husbandry.

IND. DATE: 02 Mar. 1778   CSL-010

CARPENTER, JOHN, ran away from Eliphalet Dimmick of Mansfield. John is age 18, 5' 8" tall, has short, brown hair and light blue eyes. Reward 4 pence.

IND. DATE: 30 Jul. 1787   CTC-001

CARPENTER, OLIVER - Obadiah Rhods and wife Abigail of Voluntown were tried for the murder of their apprentice Oliver Carpenter. May, 1733 - Court sent Rhods to Rhode Island.

RECORD DATED: 05 Dec. 1732   CSL-GA-08

CARPENTER, RUPEL, aged about 1 year, 8 months, child of Richard Bradock Carpenter of Bolton, bound to John Bradley of Stafford until age 15, which will be on 06 May 1816 to learn the trade of farming.

IND. DATE: 11 Jan. 1803   CSL-011

CARRINGTON, SOLOMON, of Farmington, child of David Carrington, bound to Asa Andrews of Farmington until age 21, which will be on 08 Sep. 1806 to learn the trade of japaning tin plate. Note dated 16 Apr. 1806 states that the habitual complaints of Solomon are connected with the effects of the amputation of his leg.

IND. DATE: 10 Aug. 1805   CSL-007

CUTTAR, HAMILTON, aged about 15 years, 9 months, 25 days, bound to Sylvester Lusk of Enfield for a term of 5 years, 2 months, 5 days to learn the trade of farming. Indenture made with the consent of the Managers of the Society for the Reformation of Juvenile Delinquents of New York.

IND. DATE: 05 Apr. 1828   CHS-004

CARTER, JASON, of Wethersfield, child of David Carter dec. and wife Susannah, bound to Elisha Deming of Wethersfield until January, 1781 to learn the trade of husbandry.

IND. DATE: 26 Apr. 1779   CSL-005

CASE, ASSAEL, of Wethersfield, child of Solomon Case dec. of Farmington, bound to James Mitchel of Wethersfield until age 21, which will be on 04 Aug. 1797, to learn the trade of servant.

IND. DATE: 12 Dec. 1784   CSL-005

CEZAR, ELIZA, of New London, aged about 2 1/2, bound to Sylvestor Clifford of New London until age 18 to learn how to knit and spin.

IND. DATE: 26 Jan. 1778   CSL-010

CHADWITH, THOMAS, of New London, bound to John Horton of New London for a term of 6 years, until age 21, to learn the trade of shoemaker and tanner.

IND. DATE: 04 Feb. 1771   CSL-010

CHAMBERLAIN, EDMOND of Ashford, fatherless boy - child of Sybel Chamberlain of Ashford, bound to William P. Sessions of Union until age 21, which will be on 03 Jan. 1839.

IND. DATE: 14 Sep. 1824   CSL-019M

CHAMBERLAIN, MARY, of Ashford, fatherless girl, child of Sybel Chamberlain, bound to Abijah Sessions, Jr. of Union until age 18, which will be on 18 Nov. 1834.

IND. DATE: 14 Sep. 1824   CSL-019M

CHAMBERLAIN, THADDEUS, of Mansfield, child of Alpheus Chamberlain of Mansfield, bound to (I)rad Storrs of Mansfield until age 21, which will be on 01 Aug. 1830, to learn the trade of servant.

IND. DATE: 07 May 1827   CSL-001

CHAMBERLAIN, WILLIS, of Ashford, bound to Charles Crawford of Union until age 21 to learn the trade of farming.

IND. DATE: 09 Dec. 1825   CSL-019M

CHAMPLIN, JOHN RENSELLER HYDE, of Lebanon bound to Joshua B. Clark of Lebanon until age 21, which will be on 29 Nov. 1848.

IND. DATE: 27 Apr. 1832   CSL-014

CHAMPLEN, JOHN, of New London, bound to Capt. Jeremiah Tabor of New London for term of 4 years, until age 21, to learn the trade of plain weaving.

IND. DATE: 23 Jun. 1774   CSL-010

CHAMPLAIN, JOHN, of Lebanon, bound to Charles Sweet of Lebanon until age 21, which will be on 29 Nov. 1848.

IND. DATE: 07 Mar. 1835   CSL-014

CHAPIN, SHARON PEASE, bound to Thomas Blanchard until age 21, which will be on 14 Jul. 1828 to learn the trade of turning gun stock. (Eliphalet Chapin, Justice of the Peace, Springfield, on indenture).

IND. DATE: 06 Sep. 1825   CHS-006

CHAPMAN, AARON, of Norwich, child of Mary Chapman, bound to Ebenezer Lothrup of Norwich until age 21 to learn the trade of blacksmith.

IND. DATE: 25 Mar. 1728   CSL-017M

CHAPMAN, ANDREW, of New London, child of Andrew Chapman dec., bound to Jeremiah Mason of Lebanon for a term of 11 years, 11 months, 15 days, until age 21, to learn the trade of cooper.

IND. DATE: 05 Jan. 1764   CSL-010

CHAPMAN, JOSEPH, of Norwich, aged about 9, bound to Simon Tracy of Norwich until age 16 to learn the trade of servant.

IND. DATE: 15 Jan. 1738/9   CSL-017M

CHAPPEL, COMFORT, child of Joshua Chappel dec., bound to Amos Bolles of New London for term of 8 years after the first of December next to learn the trade of cordwainer and tanner.

IND. DATE: 03 Nov. 1766   CSL-010

CHAPELL, NATHANIEL, transient person, brought before court in Litchfield to answer charges of theft by both Isaac Lawrence and Benjamin Richmond. Bound to Ebenezer Leavensworth of Woodbury for term of 5 years to satisfy 40 shilling fine.

IND. DATE: 16 Oct. 1762   LHS-001

CHAPPEL, PETER, of New London, bound to Chauncey Buckley of Colchester until age 21, which will be in July 1773, to learn the trade of hatter.

IND. DATE: 20 Feb. 1769   CSL-010

CHENEY, ALLYN, ran away from Asa Francis of Hartford. Allyn has a light complextion, short hair, hard of hearing and trained as blacksmith. Reward $8.

NEWSPAPER DATED: 17 Jun. 1793   CTC-001

CHESTER, HANNAH, of Groton, aged about 14 May last, bound to Obediah Baley of Groton until age 18 to learn the trade of housewifery.

IND. DATE: 07 Jun. 1784   ICR-001

CHILUS, LUCRETIA, of Middletown, child of Louis Phelps, bound to John Jones of Middletown until age 18, which will be on 09 Feb. 1826, to learn the trade of housewifery.

IND. DATE: 01 Apr. 1815   MHS-001

CLAP, AMOS, of Tolland, child of Nathan Clap, bound to Jonathan Hatch of Tolland until age 21, which will be on 07 Jul. 1799, to learn the trade of husbandry.

IND. DATE: 26 Dec. 1785   CSL-003

CLARK, AARON, of Windham (late of Hartford), ran away from his master, Ebiel Abbot of Windham.

RECORD DATED: 19 Apr. 1735   CHS-003

CLARK, CEMANTHA, of Farmington, bound to Chauncey Woodruff of Farmington until age 18, which will be on 13 Jul. 1828, to learn the trade of housewifery.

IND. DATE: 24 May 1825   CSL-007

CLARKE, DANIEL, of Wethersfield, child of Moses Clarke, bound to Eli Haws of Willington until age 21, which will be on 16 Jan. 1813, to learn the trade of tanning.

IND. DATE: 25 Aug. 1807   CSL-005

CLARK, ELISHA, of Hartford, with approval of guardian Benjamin Colton, bound to John Seymour as shoemaker. May 1771 John Seymour brings court action against Clark as he had enlisted with troops during term of indenture.

IND. DATE: 19 Mar. 1759   CSL-GA-02

CLARK, HARRIOT, of Farmington, illegitimate daughter of Hannah Teel, bound to Samuel Teel of Farmington until age 18, which will be on 29 Dec.1832, to learn the trade of housewifery.

IND. DATE: 01 Jan. 1819   CSL-007

CLARK, LAMBERTON, of Middletown, child of Widow Mary Foster, bound to Daniel Hall of Middletown for term of 8 years, 8 months, to learn the trade of tanner.

IND. DATE: 03 Mar. 1772   MHS-001

CLARK, LUCIUS, age 3 on 4 July 1805, bound to Eliphaz Clark of Lebanon until age 21 to learn the trade of husbandry.

IND. DATE: 24 Mar. 1806   CSL-004

CLARKE, MARY, of Bolton, aged 13 on 27th July 1831, child of Isaac Clarke dec., bound to Erastus Fuller of Hebron until age 18 to learn the trade of servant.

IND. DATE: 04 Jun. 1831   CSL-011

CLARK, MICHAEL, JR., of Middletown, child of Michael Clark, bound to Ephriam Bound of Middletown until age 21, which will be on May 10, 18( ) to learn the trade of baking.

IND. DATE: 03 Apr. 1815   MHS-001

CLEMMONS, HARVEY, ran away from William Clemmons of Granby. Harvey is small for age, has black curly hair, age 18. Reward 6 pence.

NEWSPAPER DATED: 15 Nov. 1790   CTC-001

CLIFFORD, JOHN PAUL, of Glastonbury, bound to Thaddeus Welles of Glastonbury until age 21, which will be on 15 Nov. 1845, to learn the trade of husbandry.

IND. DATE: 28 Sep. 1832   GHS-001

COLES, HARRY E., of Hartford, born 15 Dec. 1863, bound to Case Lockwood & Brainard Company of Hartford until age 21, which will be on 15 Dec. 1884, to learn the trade of book compositor.

IND. DATE: 09 Dec. 1880   CHS-001

COLE, JONATHAN, ran away from Thomas Spencer of East Hartford. Jonathan is 5' 10" tall, has black hair, fair complextion, age 20. Reward 13 pence 1/2 penny.

IND. DATE: 31 Jul. 1775   CTC-001

COLTON, AARON JR., of Springfield, Massachusetts, child of Aaron Colton, bound to Augustus Fitch of Windsor for term of 4 years to learn the trade of house joyner.

IND. DATE: 08 Feb. 1776   CHS-007

COLTON, NANCY, of Ellington, child of Horace Colton dec. of Bolton, bound to Benjamin Pinney until age 18 to learn the trade of servant.

IND. DATE: 23 Nov. 1804   CSL-011

COMBS, WILLIAM, of Wethersfield, child of Andrew Combs, bound to William Bement of Salisbury until age 21, which will be on 28 Mar. 1767, to learn the trade of blacksmith.

IND. DATE: 01 Feb. 1764   CSL-005

CONE, ELIJAH, ran away from David Townsend Jr. of Hebron. Elijah is age 17. Reward 3 pence.

NEWSPAPER DATED: 16 Jan. 1792   CTC-001

CONE, LUCINDA, of Middletown, child of Joseph and Sarah Cone, bound to Clarissa Redfield of Middletown until age 18, which will be on 25 DEC. 1809 to learn the trade of housewifery.

IND. DATE: 03 DEC. 1804   MHS-001

CONGDON, JOHN, of New London, born 17Mar.1750, child of John Congdon dec. and wife Ruth, bound to David Rogers of Norwich until age 21, which will be on 05 Mar. 1771, to learn the trade of blacksmith. Letter of indenture written by John's mother Ruth.

IND. DATE: 10 Aug. 1761   CSL-010

COOK, CASS, of New London, bound to Joseph Stubbiens of New London for term of 9 years, 15 days, until age 21, to learn the trade of shoemaker or tanner.

IND. DATE: 06 Jul. 1767   CSL-010

COOK, JOHN, of New London, aged about 15 the 16th of October last, bound to David Smith of New London for term of 5 years and 8 1/2 months, until age 21, to learn the trade of shoemaking.

IND. DATE: 06 Feb. 1769   CSL-010

COOK, MOSES, ran away from Ashbel Wells of West Hartford. Moses is age 19, 5' 4" tall, and has brown hair.

NEWSPAPER DATED: 25 Apr. 1768   CTC-001

COOKE, SARAH, of Norwich, child of William Cooke dec., bound to John Ford of Norwich until age 18 or until time of her marriage, to learn the trade of servant.

IND. DATE: 21 Jan. 1750/1   CSL-017M

COOL, LEMUEL, ran away from Nathaniel Edgerton of Salisbury. Lemuel is age 14, 5' tall, has dark brown hair, and light complection. Reward six pence.

NEWSPAPER DATED: 13 Feb. 1781   CTC-001

COOLY, CALEB, of Windham, bound to William Brewster of Windham for 2 months to satisfy debt.

IND. DATE: 05 Jul. 1758   CHS-003

COOPER, RUFUS, ran away from Ezekiel Root of Pittsfield, Massachusetts. Rufus is 5' 9" tall, trim, has curly hair, eyes are remarkably light, and is age 21. Reward $8.

NEWSPAPER DATED: 28 Sep. 1773   CTC-001

COPLEY, WILLIAM, of Harwinton, bound to Ebenezar Bolles of Litchfield. William Copley is bound to Bolles unless Bolles releases Samuel Copley, his son who is now apprentice to learn the trade of saddle making. William to pay 100 pounds for his son's release.

IND. DATE: 08 Mar. 1797   LHS-002

COREY, CAROLINE, of Ashford, parents are dead, bound to David Corey of Chaplin until age 18 to learn habits of obedience, industry and economy.

IND. DATE: 23 Sep. 1841   CSL-019M

CORY, HENRY, of Ashford, bound to Alexander Mosely of Chaplin until age 18 to learn the trade of farming.

IND. DATE: 04 Jul. 1842   CSL-019M

CORY, MASON, of Ashford, whose father is dead, bound to Ludovicios Williams of Pomfret until age 21 to learn the trade of farming.

IND. DATE: 13 Jun. 1826   CSL-019M

CORNWELL, SYLVESTER, of Middletown, child of William Cornwell, bound to Jedidiah Hubbard of Middletown until age 21, which will be on 25 Feb. 1817, to learn the trade of shoemaker.

IND. DATE: 21 May 1813   MHS-001

COTNEY, GEORGE, of Tolland, bound to Leonard Cotney for term of 7 years. Leonard Cotney agrees to remove George Cotney to Henry, Illinois for sum of $150.

IND. DATE: 03 Apr. 1866   CSL-031

COTTON, BETSEY, child of Isaac Cotton dec. of Bolton, bound to John A. Hall of Bolton until age 18 to learn the trade of servant.

IND. DATE: 03 Nov. 1804   CSL-011

COTTON, DANIEL, age 4 April last, child of Isaac Cotton dec. of Bolton, bound to John A. Hall of Bolton until age 21 to learn the trade of tanning and dressing leather.

IND. DATE: 17 Mar. 1805   CSL-011

COUCH, JOSEPH B., of Farmington, child of Amos Couch of Farmington, bound to Oliver Orvice of Farmington until age 21, which will be on 14 Dec. 1822.

IND. DATE: 09 Mar. 1818   CSL-007

CRANDALL, LYMAN WELLS, of Middletown, child of Sarah Crandall, bound to Titus Turner of Plymouth until age 21, which will be on 02 Jan. 1846, to learn the trade of farming.

IND. DATE: 22 Nov. 1833   MHS-001

CRANDLE, LYMAN, of Middletown, bound to Townsend Way of Middletown until age 21, which will be on 02 Jan. 1846, to learn the trade of paper staining.

IND. DATE: 03 Jun. 1839   MHS-001

CREIGHTON, FREDERICK A., aged 19 on 13 Jan. 1870, child of James W. Creighton, bound to Case Lockwood & Brainard Company of Hartford, until 07 Mar. 1872 to learn the trade of compositor.

IND. DATE: 16 Apr. 1870   CHS-001

CROCKER, ELIZABETH, of New London, bound to Freeman Crocker of New London for term of 8 years, 11 months, until age 18, to learn the trade of housewifery.

IND. DATE: 10 Dec. 1770   CSL-010

CROCKER, JOHN, of New London, child of Elihu Crocker dec., bound to Freeman Crocker of New London for term of 6 years, 1 month, and 24 days to learn the trade of mariner.

IND. DATE: 18 Feb. 1767   CSL-010

CROCKER, LUCRETIA, of New London, bound to Pember Calkins of New London for term of 8 years, until age 18, to learn the trade of housewifery.

IND. DATE: 05 Mar. 1770   CSL-010

CROCKER, LUCY, of New London, aged about 7, bound to Daniel Shaw of East Haddam until age 18 to learn the trade of housewifery.

IND. DATE: 06 Jan. 1779   CSL-010

CROCKER, MARY, of New London, aged 12 years last August, bound to Joseph Swan and wife Mary of Stonington to learn the trade of housewifery.

IND. DATE: 18 Dec. 1779   CSL-010

CROCKER, MEHITABLE, of New London, bound to Josephine Love(t) of New London for term of 7 years, 2 months, until age 18, to learn the trade of housewifery.

IND. DATE: 08 Feb. 1775   CSL-010

CROFMAN, JACOB, of New London, bound to Samuel H. Parsons of Lyme for term of 3 years, at age 15.

IND. DATE: 05 Jun. 1775   CSL-010

CROFSMAN, THOMAS, of New London, bound to Elijah Waterhouse of New London for term of 4 years, 8 months, until age 21, to learn the trade of house carpenter. Elijah Waterhouse to teach Thomas Crofsman how to fraim a barn and if he fail in that then give his apprentice a cow and calf.

IND. DATE: 09 Jan. 1775   CSL-010

CROMWELL, ROBERT, was born in Charleston, South Carolina, and taken to Antigua by his mother. She died and Phineas Cook of Wallingford, Connecticut took him as apprentice. Cook tried to desert Cromwell at Amboy, New Jersey. Cromwell became a cripple and Cook deserted him on an island near Long Island in 1757. Jury found Cook guilty for this as well as cruelty to apprentice Aaron Burr. 1759 Cook absconded.

RECORD DATED: 1757   CSL-GA-09

CROSLEY, ELIJAH, of Middletown, bound to Townsend Way of Middletown until age 21, which will be on 06 Jun. 1842 to learn the trade of paper staining.

IND. DATE: 03 Jun. 1839   MHS-001

CROSS, URIAH, ran away from Adoniram Grant of Tolland. Uriah is age 20, 5' 4" tall, has dark hair, thick set, left hand somewhat withered, and a scar on left hand and left elbow. Reward $10.

NEWSPAPER DATED: 05 Mar. 1770   CTC-001

CRAW, JONATHAN, charges his master, Thomas Clark of Haddam, with cruelty and wants to be discharged from service.

RECORD DATED: 07 Mar. 1728   CSL-GA-010

CROW, MARY JANE, inmate of almshouse of Farmington, child of Almira Hull, alias Andruss, alias Crow, bound to Lorin Byington of Bristol until age 18, which will be on 10 Apr. 1857, to learn the trade of housewifery.

IND. DATE: 27 Oct. 1846   CSL-007

CULVER, DANIEL, of New London, aged about 9, bound to Daniel Shaw of East Haddam until age 21.

IND. DATE: 06 Jan. 1779   CSL-010

CULVER, LUCRETIA, of New London, bound to Pearley Brown of Preston until age 18, which will be on 01 May 1789, to learn the trade of housewifery.

IND. DATE: 11 Oct. 1782   CSL-010

COLVER, REUBEN, of Litchfield, child of Joshua Colver, bound to Timothy Skinner of Litchfield until age 21 to learn the trade of joyner. (indenture unsigned).

IND. DATE: 20 Dec. 1783   LHS-001

CULVER, RICHARD, of New London, bound to Elias Fish of Preston until age 21 to learn the trade of husbandry.

IND. DATE: 12 Jul. 1779   CSL-010

CUNNINGHAM, BETSEY, of Middletown, child of Samuel Cunningham, bound to Stephen Hosmer of Middletown until age 18, which will be on 28 Mar. 1798, to learn the trade of housewifery.

IND. DATE: 02 Sep. 1796   MHS-001

CUNNINGHAM, REBECCA, of Middletown, child of Samuel Cunningham, bound to Nehemiah Hubbard, Jr. of Middletown until age 18 to learn the trade of housewifery.

IND. DATE: 07 Dec. 1795   MHS-001

CURTIS, LUMAN of Farmington, child of Alvin Curtis, bound to Mark Gridley of Farmington until age 16, which will be on 08 Apr. 1820, to learn the trade of farming.

IND. DATE: 04 Mar. 1815   CSL-007

D'OYLY, CHARLES, child of Robert D'Oyly of Adderbury West Oxford, England, bound to Samuel Tebby of Fritwell, Oxford, England for term of 7 years to learn the trade of carpenter/joiner.

IND. DATE: 02 Dec. 1817   CSL-032-M

DWOLF, SARAH of Middletown, aged about 11, child of Simon Dwolf dec., bound to Josiah Savage and wife Sarah of Middletown until age 18 to learn the trade of housewifery.

IND. DATE: 07 Sep. 1767   MHS-001

D'WOLF, STEPHEN, of Wethersfield, child of Phebe Andruss (alias Davis) and the reputed son of Stephen D'Wolf of Glastonbury, bound to Samuel Galpin of Middletown until age 21 to learn the trade of husbandry.

IND. DATE: 14 Nov. 1739   CSL-005

DAILY, CYRUS, of Farmington, illegitimate child of Hannah Teel of Farmington, bound to Samuel Teel until age 21, which will be on 11 May 1842, to learn the trade of carpenter or wheel wright.

IND. DATE: 27 May 1826   CSL-007

DANIELS, JEDIDIAH, of New London, bound to Joseph Harriss of New London until age 21.

IND. DATE: 01 Feb. 1779   CSL-010

DANIEL, JOHN, aged about 5, bound to Joseph Packer of Groton until age 21 to learn the trade of cupper liquis.

IND. DATE: 14 Apr. 1758   ICR-001

DANIELS, JONATHAN - Selectmen of the town of Hartland warned Jonathan Daniels to leave town and warned his brother, Pelatiah Daniels, to no longer entertain him.

RECORD DATED: 30 Apr. 1762   HTH-001

DANIELS, MARY of New London, bound to Amos Avery of New London until age 18 to learn the trade of weaver.

IND. DATE: 06 Jul. 1778   CSL-010

DANIELS, WILLIAM of Middletown, child of Patrick Daniels, bound to Joseph Peck of Berlin until age 21 to learn the trade of husbandry.

IND. DATE: 10 Mar. 1794   MHS-001

DARLING, GEORGE, of Bolton, aged 2 years, 15 months last May, child of Hannah Little, bound to Capt. Abner Loomis of Bolton, until age 21, to learn the trade of husbandry.

IND. DATE: 20 Nov. 1787   CSL-011

DARROW, DANIEL, of New London, child of Nicholas Darrow dec., with the approval of his guardian William Holt, bound to John Coit, Jr. of New London until 09 Feb. 1744/5 to learn the trade of ship wright.

IND. DATE: 01 May 1740   CSL-010

DART, ELIZABETH, of Bolton, child of Samuel Dart, bound to Capt. Abner Loomis of Bolton until age 18 to learn the trade of servant.

IND. DATE: 20 Nov. 1787   CSL-011

DART, GEORGE, of New London, bound to Edmond Darrow of Norwich for a term of 5 years, 3 months, and 20 days at which time he will be 21, to learn the trade of nail making/blacksmith.

IND. DATE: 02 Mar. 1778   CSL-010

DART, JAMIS, of New London, bound to John Utter of Norwich until age 21 to learn the trade of blacksmith.

IND. DATE: 01 May 1780   CSL-010

DART, JEHIAL, of Bolton, child of Samuel Dart, bound to Capt. Abner Loomis of Bolton until age 21 to learn the trade of husbandry.

IND. DATE: 20 Nov. 1787   CSL-011

DART, JERUSHA, of Bolton, child of Samuel Dart, bound to Martin Kellogg of Wethersfield until age 18 to learn the trade of servant.

IND. DATE: 12 Feb. 1787   CSL-011

DAVENPORT, JAMES, of New London, with the approval of his guardian John Owen, bound to Benjamin Rogers of New London until age 21, which will be on 14 Apr. 1800, to learn the trade of cordwainer.

IND. DATE: 15 Mar. 1795   CSL-010

DAVENPORT, RICHARD, of Coventry, child of William Davenport, bound to Abial Abbot of Windsor for term of 4 years, 2 months to learn the trade of joynor.

IND. DATE: 08 Mar. 1732   CHS-008

DAVIS, MARY, of Wethersfield, child of Samuel Davis dec. and wife Hannah, bound to Josiah Francis and wife Melisient of Wethersfield until age 18, which will be on 06 Apr. 1793, to learn the trade of housewifery.

IND. DATE: 25 Jun. 1779   CSL-033

DAVIS, RICHARD, aged 14 years, 10 months, 14 days, bound to Sylvester Lusk of Enfield for term of 6 years, 2 months, 16 days to learn the trade of farming. Indenture made with the consent of the Managers of Society for the Reformation of Juvenile Delinquents of New York.

IND. DATE: 14 Apr. 1836   CHS-004

DAVIS, ROYCE, ran away from Eliakim Deming of Farmington. Royce is 35 years old, is 5' tall, has curly, bushy, black hair, pale complextion and short flat nose. He has twice been convicted for theft. Reward $2.00.

NEWSPAPER DATED: 23 Apr. 1771   CTC-001

DAVIS, SAMUEL (alias Squier, alias Cook), of Tolland, bound to Capt. Ichabod Hinckley of Tolland until age 21 to learn the trade of husbandry.

IND. DATE: 26 Oct. 1786   CSL-003

DAWSON, WILLIAM, ran away from Epaphras Bull of Hartford. William is of Irish extract, age 30, 5' 7" tall, light hair, thin, light complextion and, grey eyes. He was apprenticed in New London, due to prosecution for theft, for term of 15 years.

NEWSPAPER DATED: 05 Mar. 1770   CTC-001

DAYTON, WILLIAM, aged about 6, bound to Joseph Chapill (the son of Jedidiah Chapill) of New London, until age 21 to learn the trade of cooper.

IND. DATE: 23 Dec. 1778   CSL-010

DEBLASIS, JOANN, aged about 17, bound to Thomas Bucior of Canton to learn the trade of housewifery.

IND. DATE: 28 Jul. 1896   APR-001

DEENS, OXENBRIDGE, of Norwich, bound to Joseph Peck to satisfy debt and learn the trade of carpenter.

IND. DATE: 02 Feb. 1787/8   CSL-017-M

DEMING, OWEN, of Wethersfield, bound to Charles Francis, Jr. of Wethersfield until age 21, which will be on 13 Aug. 1831, to learn the trade of carpenter/joiner.

IND. DATE: 18 Aug. 1828   CSL-033

DEMOND, AMASA, aged 5 on 5 April 1806, bound to Peter Anthony of Canterbury until age 21 to learn the trade of husbandry.

IND. DATE: 14 Apr. 1806   CSL-004

DENNIS, MARY, of New London, bound to Mrs. Bathsheba Smith of New London until age 18 to learn the trade of housewifery.

IND. DATE: 22 Apr. 1780   CSL-010

DENNISON, CHARLES, of Lyme, child of Esther Robbins (late Esther Dennison and then wife to Elijah Robbins) bound to Joseph Mather of Lyme until age 21, which will be on 28 Sep. 1803, to learn the trade of shoemaking and tanning. Suit against Elijah Robbins because Charles Dennison ran away from Mather 16 April 1798. Joseph Noyes of Lyme was commanded to attach the goods of Robbins of Suffield for value of $400 or attach his body to appear in County Court of Norwich on first Thursday of February 1801. Noyes attached Robbins' dwelling house, barn and 2 acres.

RECORD DATED: (27 Oct. 1795)   KML-001

DESAND, JOSHUA, ran away from Benjamin Katrane of Marlborough. Joshua is small for age, has light complection and is inclined to talk.

IND. DATE: 18 Jul. 1796   CTC-001

DEWEY, ASHBEL, of Westfield, Massachusetts, child of Esther Dewey, bound to Comfort Lane of Suffield until age 21, which will be on 19 Jun. 1816, to learn the trades of shop joiner, chairmaker and wagon builder.

IND. DATE: 28 Jan. 1813   KML-001

DICKINSON, HARVEY, of Wethersfield, bound to Samuel Larkin of Wethersfield until age 16, which will be on 03 Oct. 1839, to learn the trade of servant.

IND. DATE: 01 Mar. 1831 CSL-033

DICKINSON, STEPHEN, of Middletown, bound to Edmond Sage of Middletown until age 16 to learn the trade of farming.

IND. DATE: 03 Dec. 1832 MHS-001

DILLINGS, JESSE, of Wethersfield, child of William Dillings dec. and wife Hannah, bound to John Loveland of Wethersfield until age 21, which will be on 05 Oct. 1802, to learn the trade of shoemaking.

IND. DATE: 11 Dec. 1786 CSL-005

DILLING, SARAH, of Wethersfield, child of William Dilling and wife Desire, bound to Pelatiah Kilborn and wife Abigail of Wethersfield until age 18 to learn the trade of weaving.

IND. DATE: 12 Jun. 1750 CSL-005

DISKIL, JOHN, of New London, aged 5 years next May, bound to Ezra Moore of Lyme until age 21 to learn the trade of husbandry.

IND. DATE: 05 Feb. 1770 CSL-010

DOAN, JOHN, of Mansfield, bound to John Wood 2nd of Springfield, Massachusetts, until age 21, which will be on 15 Feb. 1832, to learn the trade of common business.

IND. DATE: 22 Oct. 1820 CSL-001

DOAN, NATHAN, of Mansfield, bound to Elijah Hammond of Ellington until age 16, which will be on 11 Sep. 1825, to learn the trade of common business.

IND. DATE: 28 Oct. 1820 CSL-001

DOAN, NATHAN, of Mansfield, bound to Lyman Wood of Springfield, Massachusetts, until age 21, which will be on 10 Sep. 1830, to learn the trade of common business.

IND. DATE: 07 Sep. 1825   CSL-001

DOBSON, ISAAC, of Wethersfield, bound to Daniel Willard of Wethersfield until age 15, which will be on 15 Oct. 1818, to learn the trade of husbandry.

IND. DATE: 02 Apr. 1817   CSL-005

DODD, JOHN, of Middletown, child of John Dodd, bound to Andrew Campbell of Middletown until age 21 to learn the trade of shoemaker.

IND. DATE: 09 Feb. 1795   MHS-001

DOOLITTLE, ENOS - Advertisement: Looking for apprentice to the Bell & Brass Foundry business - one from the country and of morals that cannot be corrupted would be preferred.

NEWSPAPER DATED: 17 Nov. 1794   CTC-001

DORCHESTER, SALLEY, of Bolton, child of Daniel Dorchester, bound to Gideon Morley of Hartford until age 14 to learn the trade of servant.

IND. DATE: 16 Sep. 1793   CSL-011

DOUGLASS, DANIEL, of New London, child of Thomas Douglass and Hannah dec., bound to Thomas Lothrup of Norwich for term of 4 years, 3 months, 5 days, to learn the trade of tanner and cordwainer.

IND. DATE: 09 Jun. 1729   CSL-017-M

DOWNER, ANDREW, bound to Elisha Edgerton of Norwich until age 21 to learn the trade of husbandman.

IND. DATE: 27 Nov. 1745   CSL-017-M

DOWNER, JOSHUA, of Norwich, child of Andrew Downer and wife Sarah of Norwich, bound to Simon Abell of Norwich until age 21 to learn the trade of tanner.

IND. DATE: 04 Apr. 1748   CSL-017-M

DOWNER, MARTHA, child of Andrew and Sarah Downer of Norwich, bound to Joseph Throop of Lebanon until age 18 to learn the trade of servant.

IND. DATE: 06 Sep. 1742   CSL-017-M

DOYLE, FRANK, of Hartford, born 07 Oct. 1864, child of John Doyle, bound to Case Lockwood & Brainard Company of Hartford until age 21, which will be on 07 Oct. 1885, to learn the trade of job pressman.

IND. DATE: 07 Oct. 1882   CHS-001

DUNBAR, BENNETT - Prisoner at Hartford County jail, petition by his attorney showing he was convicted of theft and was a minor of 13 years and was sentenced to be whipped and pay fine of $20. Dunbar has the opportunity to go on a whaling expedition and praying that his sentence may be commuted to binding into service to the master of a whaling vessel - term not exceeding 2 years and deduct from wages sufficient funds to pay fine.

RECORD DATED: May 1803   CSL-GA-011

DUNHAM, BASHEBA, of Wethersfield, child of David Dunham, bound to Elisha Wells of Wethersfield until age 18, which will be on 12 Jun. 1790, to learn the trade of servant.

IND. DATE: 21 Sep. 1787   CSL-005

DURANG, CHARLES E., of East Hartford, born 23 Apr. 1850, child of Harriet L. Durang, bound to Case Lockwood & Brainard Company of Hartford for term of 3 years to learn the trade of job pressman.

IND. DATE: 23 Sep. 1878   CHS-001

DURKEE, JEREMIAH, ran away from Nathaniel Moseley, Jr. of Windham. Jeremiah is age 17, 5' 9" tall, slightly crossed eyed, and missing left large toe. Reward $3.00

NEWSPAPER DATED: 02 Jul 1771   CTC-001

DWIGHT, MARY ANNA, of Farmington, child of Mary Andrus, bound to David H. Gleason of Farmington until age 18, which will be on 01 Jan. 1834, to learn the trade of housewifery.

IND. DATE: 27 Sep. 1819   CSL-007

EARES, JOHN, child of William Eares, bound to James Ensigne until age 21 to learn the trade of cooper. If James Ensigne does not teach John Eares a trade, then he is to give apprentice 10 pounds.

IND. DATE: 30 Dec. 1662   CSL-012-D

EATON, DANIEL, of Tolland, child of Simeon and Tabatha Eaton, bound to Benjamin Norris of Tolland until age 21 to learn the trade of husbandry.

IND. DATE: 14 Jun. 1787   CSL-003

EATON, RACHEL, of Tolland, child of Simeon Eaton, bound to Elijah Haskel of Tolland until age 18, which will be on 29 Dec. 1798, to learn "womans work".

IND. DATE: 24 Apr. 1788   CSL-003

EDGERTON, DANIEL, of Mansfield, bound to Isaac Farwell until age 21, which will be on 18 Jan. 1851, to learn the trade of husbandry.

IND. DATE: 01 Jul. 1844   CSL-001

EDGERTON, PHILA, of Mansfield, bound to Earl Swift, 2nd of Mansfield until age 18, which will be May 1849, to learn the trade of housewifery.

IND. DATE: 13 Jun. 1839   CSL-001

EDWARDS, ANNA, bound to William Gordon of Norwich until age 18, which will be on 20 Aug. 1822, to learn the trade of housekeeping.

IND. DATE: 30 May 1814   CSL-003

EDWARDS, JOHN WILKS, ran away from Daniel Comstock of Washington. John is age 19, 5' 6" tall, has light complextion, and is trained as cooper. Reward 10 dollars.

NEWSPAPER DATED: 27 Oct. 1794   CTC-001

ELLIS, NATHAN, ran away from Jessey Kimball of Canaan. Nathan is age 19, 5' 6" tall, and has darkish complextion. Reward one shilling.

NEWSPAPER DATED: 07 Jun. 1774   CTC-001

ELLIS, PHEBE, child of Joseph Ellis dec., bound to Benjamin Fitch Jr. of Norwich until age 18, or the time of her marriage, to learn the trade of servant.

IND. DATE: 28 Jan. 1750/1   CSL-017-M

ELVIN, WILLIE CONE, aged 16 on 31 Jan. 1886, child of James Elvin, bound to Case Lockwood & Brainard Company of Hartford. Term of indenture - until he is 21, which will be on 31 Jun. 1891, to learn the trade of job pressman.

IND. DATE: 02 Aug. 1886   CHS-001

ELWOOD, THOMAS J., of Hartford, born 29 Sep. 1866, child of Thomas Elwood, bound to Case Lockwood & Brainard Company of Hartford until age 21, which will be on 29 Sep. 1887, to learn the trade of job pressman.

IND. DATE: 09 Aug. 1883   CHS-001

ENSIGN, SALMON, of Westfield, Massachusetts, child of (Isaac) Ensign of Suffield, bound to John Dewey, Jr. of Suffield until age 21, which will be on 15 SEP. 1810, to learn the trade of carriage maker.

IND. DATE: 06 Aug. 1806   KML-001

EVANS, AMELIA, aged about 10 - inmate of almshouse - taken on trial by Ralph Northam of Portland to learn the trade of servant.

IND. DATE: 05 Feb. 1867   MTH-001

EVINS, SAMUEL JR., ran away from Stephen Richardson of Coventry. Samuel is 5' 7" tall, has very wide mouth, broad forehead, slender, and talks much. Reward 2 coppers.

NEWSPAPER DATED 05 May 1777   CTC-001

EVERTON, MATILDA, of Mansfield, bound to Azariah Freeman of Mansfield until age 18, which will be on 19 May 1820, to learn the trade of housewifery.

IND. DATE: 05 Feb. 1808   CSL-001

FAIRBANKS, DAVID, of Middletown, bound to Andrew Campbell of Middletown until age 21, which will be on 20 Mar. 1795, to learn the trade of shoemaker.

IND. DATE: 22 Feb. 1791   MHS-001

FARGO, AARON, of Norwich, child of Aaron Fargo, bound to Curtice Cleaveland of Norwich until age 21 to learn the trade of cordwainer and tanner.

IND. DATE: 13 Nov. 1746   CSL-017M

FARGO, ELIZABETH, of New London, child of Ralph Fargo, bound to John Hewett and wife Ruth of Norwich for term of 10 years, 9 months, 1 day to learn the trade of servant.

IND. DATE: 01 Apr. 1786   CSL-017M

FARGO, JASON, of Norwich, child of Aaron Fargo, bound to Jonathan But-
tolph of Norwich until age 21 to learn the trade of shop joynor.

IND. DATE: 26 Dec. 1747   CSL-017M

FINCH, ABRAM, aged 1 year, 10 months, child of single-woman Rose
Anna Finch of Norwich, bound to Nathaniel Philips of Windham until age 21
to learn the trade of servant.

IND. DATE: 11 Sep. 1746   CSL-017-M

FINNEY, FREDERICK, bound to Daniel Haines of Lebanon until age 21 to
learn the trade of making shoes.

IND. DATE: 26 Nov. 1798   CSL-004

FINNEY, JUSTUS, aged 10 on 2 February last, bound to Chandler Bartlett
of Lebanon until age 21.

IND. DATE: 20 Nov. 1798   CSL-004

FISHER, CHRISTOPHOR - aged about 15 years the 13th of last September,
was born in Portsmouth, England. He now resides in New London and binds
himself to Benjamin Henshaw of Middletown until age 21 to learn the trade
of seaman with the mariner art or the art of navigation.

IND. DATE: 29 Jul. 1771   CSL-010

FISHER, CHRISTOPHER, of Middletown, child of Widow Fisher, bound to
John Warren of Middletown until 01 Dec. 179(8) to learn the trade of husbandry.

IND. DATE: 25 Mar. 1793   MHS-001

FISHER, CHRISTOPHER, of Middletown, child of Widow Fisher, bound to Samuel Lee of Middletown until age 21 to learn the trade of setwork coopering.

IND. DATE: 06 Mar. 1797   MHS-001

FISHER, DAVID, of Middletown, child of Widow Bardsley, bound to Jedediah Starr, Jr. of Middletown until age 21, which will be on 29 Dec. 1803, to learn the trade of paper making.

IND. DATE: 10 Nov. 1794   MHS-001

FISHER, ELIZABETH, of Middletown, child of Christopher Fisher dec., bound to Ephriam and Beulah Merriam of Wallingford for term of 7 years to learn the trade of mantee making.

IND. DATE: 13 Oct. 1788   MHS-001

FISHER, ORRIN, of Middletown, child of Lydia Fisher, bound to Joseph Doolittle of Middletown for term of 18 years to learn the trade of joiner.

IND. DATE: 09 Nov. 1789   MHS-001

FISHER, WILLIAM, of Middletown, child of Christopher Fisher dec., bound to John Merriam of Wallingford for term of 8 years to learn the trade of farming.

IND. DATE: 09 Jun. 1788   MHS-001

FITCH, JOHN, ran away from Elisha Landon of Salisbury. John is 5' 8" tall and has short brown hair. Reward one penny.

NEWSPAPER DATED: 25 Mar. 1793   CTC-001

FLANAGAN, HIRAM, of Glastonbury, child of Barnabas Flanagan, bound to Jennant Chapman of Glastonbury until age 21, which will be on 14 Jun. 1812, to learn the trade of mariner.

IND. DATE: 27 Aug. 1801   CSL-006

FOLLEN, JOHN, of Glastonbury, bound to John Hollister of Glastonbury until age 21, which will be on 19 May 1800, to learn the trade of husbandry.

IND. DATE: 23 Mar. 1784   CSL-006

FOLLAN, THOMAS, of Glastonbury, bound to Amos Loveland late of Glastonbury, until age 21, which will be on 11 Jan. 1802, to learn the trade of husbandry.

IND. DATE: 27 Jan. 1785   CSL-006

FOLLET, WILLIAM, of New London, bound to Thomas Fo(s)dick of New London until age 21, which will be on 23 Jun. 1766, to learn the trade of blacksmith.

IND. DATE: 03 Jan. 1757   CSL-010

FORD, CORNELIA, of Farmington, bound to Solomon Porter of Hartford until age 18, which will be on 04 Oct. 1822, to learn the trade of housewifery.

IND. DATE: 12 Nov. 1818   CSL-007

FOSS, ROBERT - Petition dated 31 Aug. 1839 - Robert Foss states he was born in Derby, England 05 Apr. 1787 and came to United States in February, 1819 - he requests citizenship. Court grants request.

RECORD DATED: 31 Aug. 1839   MNT-001

FOSTER, EDWARD (JR.), of Middletown, child of Edward Foster, bound to Amos Foster of Wallingford until age 14, which will be on 30 Sep. 1806, to learn the trade of husbandry.

IND. DATE: 13 Aug. 1804   MHS-001

FOSTER, ELIZUR, of Middletown, child of Edward Foster, bound to Benjamin Merriam Jr. of Wallingford until age 15, which will be on 09 Apr. 1812, to learn the trade of husbandry.

IND. DATE: 13 Aug. 1804   MHS-001

FOX, ALBEL, ran away from Robert Sloan. Albel is age 20, has long, black hair, swarthy complextion, and an uncommon glaring look in eyes.

NEWSPAPER DATED: 08 Apr. 1776   CTC-001

FOX, THOMAS M., aged about 16 on 14 Apr. 1872, child of Mary Fox, bound to Case Lockwood & Brainard Company until age 21, which will be on 14 Apr. 1877, to learn the trade of a ruler.

IND. DATE: 17 Jun. 1872   CHS-001

FRANCIS, JOB, ran away from William Burrit of Woodbury. Job is age 19, 5' 8" tall, has long, black hair, dark eyes, and well fed. Reward one penny.

IND. DATE: 29 Mar. 1785   CTC-001

FRANCIS, JUSTUS, with approval of his guardian John Francis of Hartford County, binds himself to William Rogers of Hartford County, until age 21, which will be on 07 Jan. 1845, to learn the trade of silversmith.

IND. DATE: 13 Dec. 1838   CHS-009

FRANZISCO, JOSEPH, of New London, bound to John Crocker of New London for term of 7 years, 2 months, at which time he will be 21, to learn the trade of mariner.

IND. DATE: 05 Jun. 1769   CSL-010

FRENCH, CHARLES C., of East Hartford, born 16 Oct. 1861, child of Joseph French, bound to Case Lockwood & Brainard Company of Hartford until age 21 (which will be on 16 Oct. 1882) to learn the trade of book compositor.

IND. DATE: 03 Mar. 1879   CHS-001

FRENCH, JAMES, of New London, bound to Jedediah Chapel, Jr. of New London for term of 12 years, at which time he will be 21, to learn the trade of cooper.

IND. DATE: 06 Jul. 1767   CSL-010

FRENCH, LUCY, of Mansfield, aged between 13/14 years, bound to Christopher Hyde of Franklin until age 18 to learn the trade of housewifery.

IND. DATE: March 1819   CSL-001

FRENCH, WILLIAM, of New London, bound to Jeremiah Ross of New London for term of 4 years, 9 months - at which time he will be age 21.

IND. DATE: 06 Aug. 1770   CSL-010

FRENCH, ZERVIAH, of New London, aged about 7 years January last, child of William French dec., bound to Mary Douglass of New London until age 18 to learn the trade of housewifery.

IND. DATE: 08 Mar. 1764   CSL-010

FULLER (no first name - female child), of Glastonbury, bound to Isaac D. Bigelow of Marlborough until age 18 to learn the trade of housewifery.

IND. DATE: 08 Jan. 1818   GHS-001

FURGERSON, ASA (alias Gary), of Bolton, son of Lucy Gary, bound to Appleton Holester of Bolton until age 21 to learn the trade of shoemaking and tanning.

IND. DATE: 21 Feb. 1798   CSL-011

GALVIN, JAMES B., of Hartford, born 25 Mar. 1865, child of Patrick Galvin, bound to Case Lockwood & Brainard Company of Hartford until 10 Feb. 1887 to learn the trade of book compositor.

IND. DATE: 10 Feb. 1883   CHS-001

GARDNER, JULIUS, of Tolland, illegitimate son of Orpiah Ried, bound to Hezekiah Nye of Tolland for term of 8 years (until age 16) to learn the trade of servant.

IND. DATE: 02 Feb. 1831   CSL-003

GARDINER, ROBERT, bound to Edward Beebe until age 21.

IND. DATE: 23 Feb. 1818   WTH-001

GARDINER, THOMAS, of New London, bound to Samuel Dennison of Lyme until age 21, which will be in July 1779, to learn the trade of husbandry.

IND. DATE: 03 Sep. 1770   CSL-010

GAYLORD, WILLIAM, ran away from Noah Lane of Killingworth. William is age 16, is short, has light brown hair, blue eyes and thick set. Reward $2.

NEWSPAPER DATED: 27 Mar. 1775   CTC-001

GIBBS, ERASTUS, of Middletown, bound to Giles Meigs of Middletown until 27 Aug. 1802 to learn the trade of hat making and felt making. Indenture was made by Jonathan Wright in order to bind the minor son of his wife to Giles Meigs.

IND. DATE: 08 Feb. 1797   CSL-034-M

GIBBS, SAMUEL, of Somers, aged 17 years, 1 month, child of Josiah Gibbs dec., and with the approval of his guardian, Eldad Phelps, binds himself to David Cady of Somers for term of 3 years, ll months to learn the trade of servant.

IND. DATE: 24 Oct. 1807   CSL-035-M

GIBSON, HOWARD J., age 16 on 29 May 1885, child of William H. Gibson, bound to Case Lockwood & Brainard Company of Hartford for term of 3 years, 5 months, 14 days (at which time he will be 21) to learn the trade of book compositor

IND. DATE: 15 Mar. 1886   CHS-001

GIBSON, JAMES, of Middletown, child of Azube Marcom, bound to Asa Beach of Waterbury until age 21, which will be on 07 Feb. 1796, to learn the trade of weaver.

Author's note: Indenture reads - "bind James Gibson a minor son of Azube Marcom that was ( ) Jacob Gibson who now belongs to the family of James Marcom dec. being grandson of said James Marcom."

IND. DATE: 04 Jul. 1784   MHS-001

GIDDEONS, FESTUS, ran away from Gad Taylor of Suffield. Festus is age 18, 5' 8" tall, and is lame in his right leg.

NEWSPAPER DATED: 30 May 1796   CTC-001

GILL, SARAH, of Middletown, child of Isaac Gill dec., bound to Francis Whitmore and wife Elizabeth of Middletown until 11 Mar. 1772 to learn the trade of housewifery.

IND. DATE: 11 Mar. 1763   MHS-001

GLADDEN, IRA, of Wethersfield, bound to Elisha Wolcott of Wethersfield until age 16, which will be on 13 Apr. 1821, to learn the trade of husbandry.

IND. DATE: 02 Jan. 1815   CSL-005

GLASENDER, SALLY, of Glastonbury, bound to Capt. Joseph Goodale and wife Ruth of Glastonbury until age 18 to learn the trade of housewifery.

IND. DATE: 22 Sep. 1797   GHS-001

GLASHER, THOMAS, of Middletown, child of Elizabeth Glasher, bound to Isaac Miller of Middletown until age 15, which will be on 06 Sep. 1810, to learn the trade of farming.

IND. DATE: 04 Apr. 1803   MHS-001

GLINN, EDWARD, of Wethersfield, child of Peggy Glinn dec., bound to Frederick Griswold of Wethersfield until age 21, which will be on 12 Jul. 1805, to learn the trade of setwork.

IND. DATE: 11 Dec. 1786   CSL-005

GOFF, TIMOTHY, of Middletown, child of Alfred Goff, bound to Joseph Dart of Chatham until age 21, which will be on 24 Mar. 1834, to learn the trade of husbandry.

IND. DATE: 25 Mar. 1828   MHS-001

GOMER, FRANCIS, of Wethersfield, child of Qu(a)sh Gomer of Wethersfield, bound to Frederick Butler of Wethersfield until age 21, which will be on 28 Feb. 1802, to learn the trade of husbandry. (NOTE: Signature on indenture appears as Voash Gomer)

IND. DATE: 14 Feb. 1787   CSL-005

GOMER, GOMER, of Wethersfield, child of Quash Gomer, bound to Hezekiah Butler of Wethersfield until age 15, which will be on 26 Nov. 1793, to learn the trade of husbandry. (NOTE: Signature on indenture appears as Vuash Gomer.)

IND. DATE: 26 Sep. 1791   CSL-005

GOODRICH, ELIAS, ran away from Eli Barns of Middletown. Elias is age 18, 5' 5" tall, has short dark hair, freckled, and knows shoemaker trade. Reward 2 coppers.

NEWSPAPER DATED: 19 Aug. 1783   CTC-001

GOODRICH, ELIJAH, ran away from Elijah Cowles of Farmington. Elijah is age 18, 5' 8" tall, has black hair, light complextion, and is trained as shoemaker.

NEWSPAPER DATED: 29 Mar. 1774   CTC-001

GOODRICH, JOHN, ran away from William Crosby of Chatham. John is age 15, has light complexion, middling size, and knows stone cutter trade.

NEWSPAPER DATED: 15 Jun. 1795   CTC-001

GOODRICH, SIBBEL, of Wethersfield, child of Jemima Goodrich, bound to Josiah Robbins of Wethersfield until age 18, which will be on 31 Jan. 1792, to learn the trade of housewifery.

IND. DATE: ( )Dec. 1783   CSL-005

GRAHAM, ANNA, of Wethersfield, child of Silas Graham and Elizabeth, bound to Asa Talcott of Glastonbury until age 18, which will be on 22 Oct. 1782. Elizabeth Graham is now wife of Edward Boborn.

IND. DATE: 12 Dec. 1774   CSL-005

GREEN (unnamed), daughter of Eunice Green, bound to Jording Dodge.

IND. DATE: 10 Jan. 1774   CTH-001

GREEN, JAMES ALEXANDER, of Fairfield, child of Alexander Green, bound to David Bradley of Fairfield for a term of 6 years, 3 months to learn the trade of joyner.

IND. DATE: 20 Jun. 1744   FHS-001

GREEN, JOHN, bound to Ens. Ebenezer Baldwin for "another year".

IND. DATE: 10 May 1770   CTH-001

GREEN, JOHN, bound to Ebenezer B( ) [torn]

IND. DATE: 01 May 1769   CTH-001

GREEN, SARAH - Paid out expenses of binding out Eunice Green's child Sarah.

IND. DATE: 02 Dec. 1785   CTH-001

GREEN, WILLIAM, of Ashford, bound to James A. Adams of Ashford until age 16 to learn trade of farming.

IND. DATE: 14 Mar. 1820   CSL-019M

GREENWOOD, SAMUEL, ran away from Thomas Warner of Wethersfield. Samuel is age 14.

NEWSPAPER DATED: 26 Nov. 1798   CTC-001

GRIDLEY, SELOMA, of Farmington, child of Cloe Whitney, bound to Samuel Langdon until age 18, which will be 12 May 1813, to learn the trade of housewifery.

IND. DATE: 22 Jun. 1809   CSL-007

GRIFFIN, JOSEPH, of New London, aged about 15 February last, states he was born in Galloway, Ireland and having no one to care for him, binds himself to Benjamin Henshaw of Middletown until age 21 to learn the trade of seaman with the mariner art or art of navigation.

IND. DATE: 29 Jul. 1771   CSL-010

GRIFFIN, THOMAS, ran away from Thomas Newhall of Hartford. Thomas Griffin is age 21, 5' 9" tall, has short dark hair, full face and knows shoemaker trade.

NEWSPAPER DATED: 30 Apr. 1770   CTC-001

GRIGGS, HARRIET, of Ashford bound to Oliver Bowen of Ashford until age 18.

IND. DATE: 03 Apr. 1839   CSL-019M

GRISWOLD, DANIEL, of Middletown, child of Moses Griswold, bound to Giles Hubbard of Middletown until age 21, which will be on 10 Feb. 1800, to learn the trade of house carpenter.

IND. DATE: 13 May 1793   MHS-001

GRISWOLD, ELIZABETH - Lorenzo Warren of Farmington pays penal sum of $500 to Selectmen of Farmington because of his fathering a female child with Elizabeth Griswold. Child born 11 Mar. 1852.

RECORD DATED: 27 Mar. 1852   CSL-007

GRO(V)EN, HOMER, child of Ebenezer Gro(v)en, bound to Henry Straight of Tolland for term of 2 years. Henry Straight takes indenture for payment of $20 per year.

IND. DATE: 11 Sep. 1834   CSL-003

GURLEY, FANNY, of Mansfield, bound to Joshua Parker of Mansfield until age 18, which will be on 22 Oct. 1825, to learn the trade of housewifery.

IND. DATE: May 1812   CSL-001

GURLEY, ROYAL OLADINE, of Mansfield, bound to Daniel Dimmick of Coventry until age 21, which will be on 30 Jun. 1831, to learn the trade of farming.

IND. DATE: 05 Jun. 1815   CSL-001

GUTHRIE, THOMAS, ran away from Isaac Parish of Washington. Thomas is 17, 5' 8" tall, dark complextion, and walks stooping. Reward 9 pence.

NEWSPAPER DATED: 09 Apr. 1787   CTC-001

HADLOCK, REUBEN, ran away from William Weare of Hartford. Reuben is 5', 5" tall, has curly hair, and light complextion. Reward 2 coppers.

NEWSPAPER DATED: 14 Mar. 1796   CTC-001

HALDEN, HARRIET, of Glastonbury, bound to Joseph Strong of South Hadley until age 18, which will be on 15 Jun. 1819, to learn the trade of housewifery.

IND. DATE: 18 Dec. 1810   GHS-001

HALE, HENRY - prisoner of Hartford jail, petition by his attorney showing he was convicted of theft and a minor of 17 years - was whipped and fined $20. Praying sentence be instead binding into service for 2 years and deduct from his wages to pay fine.

RECORD DATED: 27 May 1803   CSL-GA-012

HAMLIN, ELIZA ELMINA, of Farmington, child of Noah Hamlin, bound to Henry Gridley of Bristol until age 18, which will be on 22 Feb. 1862, to learn the trade of farming.

IND. DATE: 26 Apr. 1849   CSL-007

HAMMOND, ISAAC, of New London, child of Widow Charity Hammond, bound to Ebenezar Weeks of New London until age 21, which will be 18 May 1778, to learn the trade of cooper.

IND. DATE: 01 Apr. 1765   CSL-010

HAMMOND, SAMUEL, ran away from Ephriam Pabodie of Norwich, New York. Samuel is 5' 9" tall, dark complextion, and thick lips. Reward - one cent.

[Samuel Hammond placed the following in the *Norwich Journal* in answer to the runaway announcement:]

"To the Public - That little man, with a little body, a littlemind, and a little cocked up nose, Ephriam Pabodie has advertised me as a runaway. I served my time out before I left him, and put up with his insults, and all the disagreeable arising from a too frequent use of the bottle. What moved the little fellow to advertise me, I cannot tell, but suppose he had a "bad advisor", viz: a whiskey bottle."

NEWSPAPER DATED: 14 May 1818   NJN-001

HAMMOND, SIBELL, of New London, child of Elijah Hammond, bound to John Bradford and wife Mary of New London for term of 6 years, 6 months at which time she will be 18 to learn the trade of housewifery.

IND. DATE: 01 Dec. 1766   CSL-010

HANABALL, JOB, of Glastonbury bound to Joseph Goodale of Glastonbury until age 21, which will be on 05 Jan. 1832, to learn the trade of husbandry.

IND. DATE: 06 Jan. 1817   GHS-001

HARRIS, DAVID, ran away from Eliphas Spencer of Salisbury. David is age 19, 5' 6" tall, and face is pock marked. Reward 5 shillings.

NEWSPAPER DATED: 12 Jun. 1781   CTC-001

HARRIS, HENRY, of Glastonbury, bound to John Hollister of Glastonbury until age 21, which will be on 15 Apr. 1797, to learn the trade of clothier.

IND. DATE: 04 Feb. 1785   CSL-006

HA(RR)Y, SALLY, of Middletown, child of James Ha(rr)y, bound to Nathan Wetmore of Haddam until age 18, which will be on 22 Nov. 1811, to learn the trade of housewifery.

IND. DATE: 09 May 1796   MHS-001

HART, HENRY, of Farmington, bound to Daniel Prindle of Simsbury until age 21, which will be on 28 Jan. 1833, to learn the trade of blacksmith.

IND. DATE: 23 Feb. 1829   CSL-007

HART, JULIA, of Farmington, child of Lucinda Hart, bound to unnamed person until age 18. [Indenture undated, unfinished, unsigned].

IND. DATE (1840)   CSL-007

HART, OZIAS, ran away from James Kilbourn of Hartford. Ozias is age 20, 5', 4" tall, has short black hair, and dark complextion. Reward $10.

NEWSPAPER DATED: 06 Apr. 1789   CTC-001

HART, POMRY HAYS, of Farmington, child of Selah Hart, bound to Titus Bidwell of Farmington until age 21, which will be on 13 Sep. 1807, to learn the trade of tin making.

IND. DATE: 11 Oct. 1802   CSL-007

HAWLEY, AMOS - Selectmen of Farmington agree to pay Elijah Hawley for supporting his son Amos $1.00 per week from 15 Apr. 1811 to 24 Jan. 1814.

IND. DATED: 24 Jan. 1814   CSL-007

HAYES, SAMUEL, of Plainfield, with the approval of his guardian Joseph Hayes, bound to Samuel Bradley of Fairfield until age 21, which will be on 16 Mar. 1812, to learn the trade of joyner.

IND. DATE: 02 Mar. 1809   FHS-001

HENDERSON, JOHN JR. of Kent, child of John Henderson, bound to Samuel Folsom of Stratford.

IND. DATE: ( )Oct. 1753   CSL-GA-003

HENRY, PRUDENCE, of Middletown, child of Widow Lydia Burdsley, bound to Christopher Fisher of Middletown until age 18, which will be on 15 Dec. 1815, to learn the trade of housewifery.

IND. DATE: 08 Aug. 1803   MHS-001

HERRICK, LUTHER, child of Rufus Herrick, bound to John Carver until age 21.

IND. DATE: 16 Oct. 1820   CTH-002

HERRICK, LYDIA, child of Rufus Herrick, bound to John Barstow, Jr..

IND. DATE: 05 Feb. 1821   CTH-002

HEWET, MARY, of New London, bound to William Gorton and wife Phebe for term of 9 years, 1 month, until age 18, to learn the trade of housewifery.

IND. DATE: 02 Aug. 1773   CSL-010

HIGBE, SAMUEL, of Middletown, child of Samuel Higbe, bound to Titus Merriman of Wallingford for term of 6 years to learn the trade of shoemaker.

IND. DATE: 11 May 1778   MHS-001

HIGBY, TIMOTHY, of Middletown, aged 12 years, 3 months, 14 days, is the child of Samuel Higby who has gone to parts unknown. Timothy is bound to Josiah Starr of Middletown until age 21 to learn the trade of tailor.

IND. DATE: 02 Nov. 1778   MHS-001

HILLS, EDWIN, of Farmington, bound to Frederick Andrus until age 21, which will be on 28 Mar. 1828, to learn the trade of shoemaker.

IND. DATE: 08 Feb. 1819   CSL-007

HILLS, ELIJAH, of Farmington, bound to Michael Barber of Farmington until age 21, which will be in January 1809, to learn the trade of shop joining.

IND. DATE: 11 Nov. 1805   CSL-007

HILLS, HEZEKIAH - Selectmen of the town of Hartland warned Hezekiah Hills to leave town with his family.

RECORD DATED: 06 Jul. 1762   HTH-001

HILL, ISAAC, bound to Stephen Keyes of Pomfret for 6 months, beginning 18 months after 10 Feb. 1761, to satisfy debt.

IND. DATE: 10 Feb. 1761   CHS-003

HILLS, MERVIN, child of Abijah Hills of Lebanon, bound to Asahel Kingsley of Columbia until age 17, which will be on 22 Apr. 1832, to learn the trade of farming.

IND. DATE: 30 Apr. 1821   CSL-004

HINMAN, HELEN, of Farmington, bound to Grove Catlin of Litchfield until age 18 to learn the trade of housewifery.

IND. DATE: 25 Apr. 1828   CSL-007

HINSON, WILLIAM, of Norwich, child of Sarah Hinson (alias Hough), bound to John Lothrup, Jr. of Norwich until age 21 to learn the trade of husbandman.

IND. DATE: 17 Jan. 1731/2   CSL-017-M

HODGES, EPHRAIM D., of Mansfield, bound to Ephraim Hodges of Mansfield until age 21, which will be on 26 Feb. 1827, to learn the trade of husbandry.

IND. DATE: 07 Mar. 1808   CSL-001

HODGES, POLLY, of Mansfield, bound to John U. Parker of Mansfield until age 18, which will be on 29 Mar. 1822, to learn the trade of housewifery.

IND. DATE: 07 Mar. 1808   CSL-001

HODGE, SUSANNA, of Lyme bound to Samuel Collins, Jr. and wife Mary of Middletown until age 18, to learn the trade of servant.

IND. DATE: 07 Jun. 1692   CSL-GA-004

HODGE, SUSANNA, of Newport, Rhode Island, child of John Hodge, bound to Joseph Butler of Wethersfield until age 18 to learn the trade of servant.

IND. DATE: 14 Jul. 1691   CSL-GA-004

HOFMAN, JOHN, Hanoverian, ran away from Jeremiah Wadsworth of Hartford. John is age 50, is 6' tall, has black with grey hair, and sore eyes. John was in the British army in America - was taken prisoner - lived with Col. Beddle in Philadelphia and was exchanged - went home and returned to New York in summer 1785. Reward $10.

NEWSPAPER DATED: 25 Sep. 1786   CTC-001

HOLLISTER, GILES, ran away from Charles Smith of Glastonbury. Giles is age 18, 5' 10" tall, and has light complextion.

NEWSPAPER DATED: 08 Aug. 1796   CTC-001

HOLMES, ABIJAH, of Bedford, New York. Writ by Thomas Fitch, assistant sheriff of New Haven, to apprehend Abijah Holmes late of Bedford, New York, to answer complaint of Jeremiah Peck, Jr. of Milford. Holmes was bound to Peck but ran off on 30 Apr. 1750 with indentures and sum of money.

Return of sheriff, dated 15 May 1750, showing he brought Holmes before Nathan Baldwin, J.P. Milford.

RECORD DATED: 07 May 1750   CSL-020-M

HOLMES, ELKANAH, of Canterbury, bound to Ruben Darbes of Canterbury for term of 5 years to satisfy debt.

IND. DATE: 19 May 1755   CHS-004

HOOKER, WILLIAM, ran away from Abijah Flagg of Hartford. William is age 17, 5' 9" tall, has long black hair, black eyes, and dark complection. Reward $5.

NEWSPAPER DATED: 29 Aug. 1796   CTC-001

HOPKINS, ANSON, of Farmington bound to Levi Hawley of Canton until age 21, which will be on 21 May 1822, to learn the trade of shoemaker/tanner.

IND. DATE: 01 Apr. 1819   CSL-007

HORNER, GEORGE - Certificate dated 22 Nov. 1817 by William Goodrich releasing George Horner as apprentice.

RECORD DATED: 22 Nov. 1817   CSL-005

HORNER, GEORGE, of Wethersfield, bound to Lyman Collins of Meriden until age 21, which will be on 03 Jul. 1828, to learn the trade of husbandry.

IND. DATE: 13 Apr. 1818   CSL-005

HORNER, MARGARET, of Wethersfield, child of Thomas Horner dec., bound to William Warner Jr. and wife Eunice of Wethersfield until age 18, which will be on 16 Dec. 1772, to learn the trade of housewifery.

IND. DATE: 19 Nov. 1763   CSL-005

HORTON, JOHN, ran away from Nehemiah Dodge of Pomfret. John is age 19, 5' 6" tall, has long black hair and dark complection. Reward 6 pence.

NEWSPAPER DATED: 22 Sep. 1794   CTC-001

HOSMER, MARTIN, ran away from Thomas Converse of Hartford. Martin is age 17, 5' 6" tall, has dark eyes, and light complextion. Reward 13 pence.

NEWSPAPER DATED: 02 Oct. 1773   CTC-001

HOWE, ALLIN, son of John Howe, was born in Watertown in a house belonging to Joel Hungerford. Deposition of Ephraim Howe of Paris County, Oneida, New York, dated 09 Jul. 1808 - Superior Court of Litchfield. Ephraim stated that Allin Howe was bound by Selectmen of Watertown to Nathaniel Bradley of Watertown until age 14. Bradley let Allin to Amos Jr. about 1798. Ephraim then took guardianship of the boy and since has bound him to a shoemaker in Washington.

RECORD DATED: 09 Jul. 1808   LHS-008

HEBARD, EBENEZAR, of Windham, bound to Capt. James Lased of Windham for a term of 2 months, 2 days to satisfy debt.

IND. DATE: 21 Jan. 1761   CHS-003

HUBBARD, F. SHERWOOD, child of Frederick W. Hubbard of Middletown, was born 09 Nov. 1865. Bound to Case Lockwood & Brainard Company of Hartford until 01 Oct. 1885 to learn the trade of job compositor.

IND. DATE: 01 Oct. 1882   CHS-001

HUBBARD, GEORGE, of Glastonbury, child of Elizabeth Hubbard, bound to Maj. Theodore Woodbridge of Glastonbury until age 21 to learn the trade of field husbandry.

IND. DATE: 18 Sep. 1787   GHS-001

HIBARD, JOSIAH, of Windham was bound to Timothy Larrabe of Windham for term of 1 year to satisfy debt.

IND. DATE: 06 Feb. 1761   CHS-003

HULL, FANNY, of Farmington, child of Isaac Hull, bound to Richard E. Goodwin of Hartford until age 18, which will be on 03 Aug. 1824, to learn the trade of housewifery.

IND. DATE: 25 Dec. 1815   CSL-007

HULL, HENRY JOSEPH, of Farmington, bound to Winthrop M. Wadsworth of Farmington until age 21, which will be on 15 Apr. 1848, to learn the trade of farming.

IND. DATE: 04 Nov. 1836   CSL-007

HULL, JOHN, of Middletown, child of Tristrum Hull, bound to Alpheus Shumway of Middletown until age 21, which will be on 24 Nov. 1811, to learn the trade of saddlery.

IND. DATE: 11 Feb. 1805   MHS-001

HULL, STEPHEN - In the year 1776 Stephen Hull was bound as apprentice to Capt. Henry Slo(f)son of Lower Salem, West Chester County, New York, as blacksmith. In 1777, with consent of master, he enlisted as fifer for term of 6 months with Capt. Pardy. In deposition Stephen Hull states he was born in Ridgefield, Fairfield County, Connecticut 06 Jul. 1762.

DEPOSITION DATED: 30 Mar. 1833   XRW-001

HULL, WALTER, of Farmington, bound to Ezekiel Andrews of Berlin until age 21, which will be on 15 Apr. 1838, to learn the trade of wheelwright.

IND. DATE: 15 Apr. 1828   CSL-007

HULL, WILLIAM, of Farmington, because of his idleness and mismanagement, bound to Frederick Andrus of Farmington for term of 6 months to learn the trade of husbandry.

IND. DATE: 13 Jun. ( )   CSL-007

HUMPHREY, WILLIAM, of Wethersfield, bound to Lathrop Richardson of Wethersfield until age 16, which will be on 04 Apr. 1828, to learn the trade of servant.

IND. DATE: 01 Apr. 1822   CSL-005

HUNTER, HANNAH, of Wethersfield, bound to William Deming of Wethersfield until age 18, which will be on 26 Dec. 1832, to learn the trade of servant.

IND. DATE: 03 Apr. 1826   CSL-005

HUNTER, MARY, of Wethersfield, child of Roswell Hunter, bound to Clarrissa Goodrich of Wethersfield until age 18 to learn trade of servant.

IND. DATE: 01 Jun. 1827   CSL-005

HURLBUT, THADDEUS, ran away from Amasa Parker of Washington. Thaddeus is age 18, 5' 8" tall, has light, short, curly hair, light eyes, and light complextion. Reward 4 pence.

NEWSPAPER DATED: 02 Jan. 1786   CTC-001

HYDE, CHARLES, of Lebanon, child of Amasa Hyde, bound to George Way of Colchester.

IND. DATE: 1840/41   CSL-004

HYDE, ELIZABETH, of Lebanon, child of Amasa Hyde, bound to David Holmes of Lebanon until age 18, which will be on 09 Dec. 1852, to learn the trade of housewifery.

IND. DATE: 24 Jan. 1842   CSL-014

HYDE, ELIZABETH, of Lebanon, bound to John Champlin, Jr. of Lebanon until age 18, which will be on 09 Dec. 1852, to learn the trade of housewifery.

IND. DATE: 20 Nov. 1843   CSL-014

HYDE, JOHN, of Lebanon, child of Amasa Hyde, bound to Roger Bailey of Lebanon until age 16, which will be on 08 Nov. 1853, to learn the trade of agriculture.

IND. DATE: 15 Sep. 1845   CSL-014

HYDE, PHINEAS, of Lebanon, child of Amasa Hyde, bound to James Webster of Lebanon until age 21, which will be on 09 Jul. 1852, to learn the trade of agriculture.

IND. DATE: 08 Dec. 1840   CSL-014

INGRAHAM, DANIEL, age 19, ran away from Simeon Dunham of Hebron. Reward one cent.

NEWSPAPER DATED: 05 Nov. 1798   CTC-001

INGRAHAM, NED, of Middletown, child of (Sall) Ingraham, bound to Asher Miller of Middletown until age 21, which will be on 10 Dec.1813, to learn the trade of husbandry.

IND. DATE: 14 Nov. 1796   MHS-001

ISHMAEL, CHLOE, of Middletown bound to Jedidiah Sage of Berlin until age 18 to learn the trade of housewifery.

IND. DATE: 09 Feb. 1795   MHS-001

JACKSON, PAMELIA, of Farmington bound to Norman Hart of Berlin until age 18, which will be on 14 May 1831, to learn the trade of servant.

IND. DATE: 26 Apr. 1819   CSL-007

JEFFORDS, BENJAMIN, aged 8 years the twenty second day of August next, child of Joseph Jeffords of Preston, bound to Samuel Killam Jr. of Preston until age 21 to learn the trade of husbandry.

IND. DATE: 12 Jan. 1770   CHS-010

JENNINGS, ISRAEL, of Wethersfield, child of Hannah Butler, bound to Elisha Stoddard of Wethersfield until age 14, which will be on 11 May 1788, to learn the trade of servant.

IND. DATE: 19 May 1783   CSL-005

(J)GENNINGS, JOHN, of Hartford, bound to Jeremiah Adams and wife Sarah for term of 7 years from 7 December 1661.

IND. DATE: 05 Dec. 1661   CSL-012-C

(J)GENNINGS, JOSEPH, bound to Richard Treat Senr. for term of 10 years. In case Treat dyes, boy is to go to any of Treat's 3 sons whom the boy doth choose.

IND. DATE: 05 Dec. 1661   CSL-012-C

JENNINGS, LOIS, of Mansfield, bound to Julius Deming of Litchfield until age 18 to learn the trade of housewifery.

IND. DATE: 22 Oct. 1823   CSL-001

JOHNS, EUNICE (alias Daniels), bound to John Watrous of Waterford.

IND. DATE: 30 Mar. 1829   WTH-001

JOHNSON, ( ) - Court approves of Goody Johnson binding her son as apprentice to [left blank] in Stratford provide master give son 20 pounds at end of term.

RECORD DATED: 28 Mar. 1650   CSL-012-F

JOHNSON, BETSEY, otherwise known as Betsey Edwards, bound to Thomas Shaw Perkins.

IND. DATE: 31 May 1824   WTH-001

JOHNSON, ELIZA, of Farmington, child of Widow Lucinda Burr, bound to Elias Dunham of Barkhamsted until age 18, which will be on 30 Jun. 1823, to learn the trade of housewifery.

IND. DATE: 20 Jun. 1809   CSL-007

JOHNSON, HARRY, of Guilford, bound to Daniel Collins of Guilford until age 21, which will be on 09 Sep. 1826, to learn the trade of servant.

IND. DATE: 08 Nov. 1813   GFL-001

JOHNSON, JAMES JR., of Wethersfield, child of James Johnson, bound to Samuel Smith of Hartford until age 21, which will be on 29 Jan. 1808, to learn the trade of sadler.

IND. DATE: 06 Apr. 1802   CSL-005

JOHNSON, JOSEPH, "lately from within the lines of the enemy", bound to John Graham of Wethersfield until age 21, which will be on 05 Feb. 1786 to learn the trade of shop and house joiner.

IND. DATE: 06 Mar. 1780   CSL-005

JONA, AZUBAH, of Glastonbury, bound to Joseph Hollister and wife Bethiah of Glastonbury until age 18, which will be on 08 Mar. 1805, to learn the trade of spinning.

IND. DATE: 21 Dec. 1789   CSL-006

JONES, AMOS, ran away from Eleazar Carter of Colchester, Amos is age 19, middling size, and has red hair. Reward 6 pence.

NEWSPAPER DATED: 21 May 1792   CTC-001

JONES, EDWARD, of Willingborough, Northampton, England - Agreement between William Leete of Keystone County of Huntington, England and Edward Jones, a carpenter of Willingborough County, England to do carpenter work in new plantation in Guilford, Connecticut. Indenture provide their joining a ship in London for Jones' passage to Quinnipiack and 3 years of service.

IND. DATE: 13 Apr. 1639   CSL-036M

JOURDAN, JEREMY, of Lebanon, child of John Jourdan, bound to Cyrus Williams of Lebanon until age 21, which will be on 04 Jul. 1852, to learn the trade of farming.

IND. DATE: 20 Aug. 1838   CSL-004

JUSTIN, NATHAN, child of Mary Justin, bound to Gideon Carver.

IND. DATE: 07 Feb. 1777   CTH-001

KAPPLE, FITCH, child of Thomas Kapple, bound to James Randall of Lebanon to learn the trade of blacksmithing.

IND. DATE: 06 Apr. 1804   CSL-004

KAPPLE, THOMAS JR., bound to Nathan Walworth of Lebanon until age 21, which will be on 13 Oct. 1808, to learn the trade of tanning and shoemaking.

IND. DATE: 01 May 1801   CSL-004

KELLY, LYDIA, of New London, bound to James Dennison and wife Esther of New London for term of 9 years, 5 months to learn the trade of housewifery.

IND. DATE: 05 Feb. 1770   CSL-010

KENT, EARL, of Suffield, child of John Kent, bound to Gad Taylor of Suffield until age 21 to learn the trade of blacksmith.

IND. DATE: 01 Feb. 1797   KML-001

KIDDER, JULIANN, of Mansfield, bound to Joseph Hull of Enfield, Massachusetts, until age 18, which will be on 31 Aug. 1857, to learn the trade of housewifery.

IND. DATE: 01 Apr. 1845   CSL-001

KILBORN, MOLLY, of Middletown, aged 6 next June, child of Hannah Burto (Presto), bound to Daniel Sumner of Middletown until age 18 to learn the trade of housewifery. Molly now belongs to the family of Hannah.

IND. DATE: 06 Apr. 1780   MHS-001

KING, EDWARD J., of Hartford, born 29 Aug. 1862, bound to Case Lockwood and Brainard Company until age 21, which will be on 29 Aug. 1883, to learn the trade of job compositor.

IND. DATE: 04 Oct. 1880   CHS-001

KNAPS, HANOVER M., of Middletown, child of William Knaps, bound to John Wilson of N. Haven until age 21 to learn the trade of blacksmith.

IND. DATE: 04 Mar. 1814   MHS-001

KNAPS, HANOVER, of Middletown, child of William Knaps, bound to Richard Graves of Middlebury until age 21, which will be on 11 Sep. 1819, to learn the trade of blacksmith.

IND. DATE: 13 May 1816   MHS-001

KNAPS, JAMES, of Middletown, child of James Knaps, bound to William Brewster of Lebanon until age 21, which will be on 28 Dec. 1840, to learn the trade of husbandry.

IND. DATE: 04 Mar. 1833   MHS-001

KNAP, MARY, of New London, bound to Richard Harris of New London until age 18 to learn the trade of housewifery.

IND. DATE: 15 Dec. 1762   CSL-010

KNAPS, WILLIAM F., of Middletown, child of William Knaps dec., bound to Nathan Wilcox of Middletown until age 21, which will be on 02 Mar. 1821, to learn the trade of chair and wagon maker.

IND. DATE: 13 May 1816   MHS-001

LAMB, ANNE of Glastonbury, child of Thomas Lamb dec., bound to Capt. Peter Burnham and wife Elizabeth of Wethersfield until age 18, which will be on 08 Mar. 1785, to learn the trade of servant.

IND. DATE: 22 Jun. 1779   CSL-006

LAMB, JOSEPH, of Glastonbury, bound to Seth Stanley of Berlin until age 21 to learn the trade of husbandry.

IND. DATE: 20 Sep. 1791   CSL-006

LAMB, THOMAS, of Glastonbury, child of Joseph Lamb dec., bound to William Warner of Wethersfield until age 21, which will be on 28 Oct. 1786, to learn the trade of husbandry.

IND. DATE: 12 Oct. 1781   CSL-006

LANDRES, SARAH, of Wethersfield, child of Samuel Landres and wife Sarah, bound to Lydia Buck until age 18 to learn the trade of housewifery.

IND. DATE: ( ) Dec. 1777   CSL-005

LANDRES, SARAH, of Wethersfield, child of Samuel Landres and wife Sarah, bound to Amos Buck and wife Abigail of Wethersfield until age 18, which will be on 18 Feb. 1782, to learn the trade of housewifery.

IND. DATE: 18 Feb. 1782   CSL-005

LANE, ISAAC, ran away from Jacob Wood of Chatham. Isaac is age 19, 5' 3" tall, has darkish complextion. One of his legs is much shorter than other. He is trained as taylor.

NEWSPAPER DATED: 24 May 1774   CTC-001

LARABY, ASA, of New London, bound to Amos Culver of New London until age 21, which will be on 15 Apr. 1787, to learn the trade of weaving.

IND. DATE: 04 Apr. 1774   CSL-010

LARRIBEE, JOHN, ran away from Joseph Forward of Granby. John is age 18, middling size and has a light complextion. Reward 2 cents.

NEWSPAPER DATED: 05 Mar. 1798   CTC-001

LATHROP, JOSEPH, of Middletown, child of Zebuliah Lathrop, bound to Jonathan Hall of Middletown until age 15, which will be on 15 Feb. 1811, to learn the trade of husbandry.

IND. DATE: 12 Nov. 1804   MHS-001

LATIMORE, MARY, of New London, child of Sarah Wright of Lyme, bound to Elizabeth Stocker of New London for term of 13 years, 9 months, 8 days, at which time she will be 18, to learn the trade of housewifery.

IND. DATE: 23 Jul. 1762   CSL-010

LEACH, AMOS, age 16, bound to John Cary of Windham.

IND. DATE: 16 Jun. 1803   WTH-001

LEACH, CHRISTOPHER, of New London, bound to John Gorton and wife Mary of New London for term of 9 years, 4 months, at which time he will be age 21, to learn the trade of weaver.

IND. DATE: 02 Feb. 1767   CSL-010

LEECH, CHRISTOPHER, of New London, bound to Benjamin Comstock of New London for a term of 2 years, 1 month, 27 days, at which time he will be age 21, to learn the trade of husbandry.

IND. DATE: 05 Apr. 1774   CSL-010

LEACH, DANIEL, ran away from Jeremiah Covert of Colebrook. Daniel is 5' 6" tall, has long, brown hair with whitish ends (much resembles a woodchuck). Trained as clothier. Reward 3 pence.

NEWSPAPER DATED: 09 May 1796   CTC-001

LEDGARD, NORMAN CHAUNCY, of Farmington, child of Truman Ledgard, bound to Cotton Kellogg of New Hartford until age 21, which will be on 13 Sep. 1833.

IND. DATE: 26 Oct. 1813   CSL-007

LEE, BENJAMIN, of Middletown, child of Samuel Lee, bound to Joseph Driggs Jr. of Middletown until age 21 to learn the trade of shoemaker.

IND. DATE: 19 Nov. 1787   MHS-001

LEE, DANIEL WILSON, of Middletown, child of Bliss Lee, bound to Elizur Barnes of Middletown until age 21, which will be on 21 Jul. 1819, to learn the trade of cabinet maker.

IND. DATE: 06 Sep. 1813   MHS-001

LEE, MARTHA, of Farmington, bound to Noah Porter of Farmington until age 18, which will be on 21 Jan. 1849, to learn the trade of housewifery.

IND. DATE: 04 Nov. 1836   CSL-007

LEE, RHODA, of Middletown, child of Samuel Lee, bound to Nehemiah Hubbard Jr. of Middletown until age 18, which will be on 28 Feb. 1813, to learn the trade of housewifery.

IND. DATE: 14 Feb. 1803   MHS-001

LEE, WILLIAM, of Middletown, child of Bliss Lee, bound to Samuel Paddock of Meriden until age 15, which will be on 28 Jun. 1815, to learn the trade of farming.

IND. DATE: 08 Mar. 1813   MHS-001

LEMING, AARON - John Guilford Collins suit with Abraham Bradley for entertaining his runaway apprentice Aaron Leming Mar. 1701.

Bradley claims Collins threatened to horse whip Leming and also did not train Leming. Bradley states he acted as guardian to his wife's brother. Court sent Leming back to Collins.

RECORD DATED: 17 Mar. 1701   CSL-GA-013

LEWIS, LEVI, ran away from Job Lewis of Southington. Levi is age 18, tall with brown hair. He knows shoemaker trade. Reward $8.

NEWSPAPER DATED: 07 Jan. 1793   CTC-001

LEWIS, MARY ANN, of Tolland, bound to Shubael Dimock of Willington until age 18 to learn the trade of servant.

IND. DATE: 30 Sep. 1832   CSL-003

LEWIS, NABOTH, ran away from Samuel Thompson. Naboth is age 18, thick set, well built, and has reddish complexion. Trained as joiner. Reward $2.

NEWSPAPER DATED: 21 Jun. 1774   CTC-001

LINCH, GABRIEL, stated that Andrew Sandford conducted fraudulent dealings in apprenticeship agreement and did not teach him two trades.

RECORD DATED: 01 Sep. 1659   CSL-012B

LOOMIS, ALEXANDER, of Lebanon, aged 17 on March 4 instant, child of Elijah Loomis, bound to Bezaleel Fuller of Lebanon until age 21, which will be on 09 Mar. 1789, to learn the trade of tanning and shoemaking.

IND. DATE: 09 Mar. 1789   CSL-004

LOOMIS, ANDREW, of Bolton, aged about 5, child of David Loomis, bound to Salmon Loomis of Bolton until age 21 to learn the trade of farming.

IND. DATE: 16 Dec. 1813   CSL-011

LOOMIS, CHARLES LEWIS, of Bolton, aged 18 on 17 Apr. 1835, bound to Thaddeus Billings of Longmeadow, Massachusetts, until age 21, to learn the trade of servant.

IND. DATE: 08 Apr. 1835   CSL-011

LOOMIS, ELECTA, of Bolton, aged about 10, bound to Edwin Skinner of Bolton until age 18 to learn the trade of housewifery.

IND. DATE: 20 Jan. 1825   CSL-011

LOOMIS, ELIJAH JR., of Lebanon, child of Elijah Loomis, bound to Salmon Champion of Lebanon until age 16. [term of two years crossed out].

IND. DATE: 15 Apr. 1782   CSL-004

LOOMIS, FREEMAN, of Lebanon, bound to Samuel Loomis of Hebron for term of two years to learn the trade of hatter. During the term of indenture, Freeman has the privilege of making 15 hats for his own benefit.

IND. DATE: 29 Mar. 1804   CSL-004

LOOMIS, JESSE, of Bolton, aged about 4, bound to Leonard Jones of Bolton until age 21 to learn the trade of farming.

IND. DATE: 16 Dec. 1813   CSL-011

LOOMIS, LUCIUS, of Middletown, child of Asahel Loomis, bound to David Dension of Middletown for term of one year to learn the trade of merchandising.

IND. DATE: 06 Nov. 1820   MHS-001

LOOMIS, SAMSON, aged about 12 on July 8 next, bound to Asa Torrey of Lebanon until age 21 to learn the trade of blacksmith.

IND. DATE: 17 Mar. 1794   CSL-004

LOOMIS, SAMUEL, of Bolton, bound to Ira Theeney of Manchester until age 21, which will be on 01 Jun. 1834, to learn the trade of shoemaking. Ira Theeney is also to see that Samuel Loomis has schooling for 6 months at Osborns Seminary in Manchester.

IND. DATE: 20 Apr. 1829   CSL-011

LOTHRUP, BETHIA, child of John Lothrup of Norwich, bound to Benjamin Lothrup and wife Mary of Norwich until age 18 to learn the trade of servant.

IND. DATE: 21 Mar. 1739   CSL-017M

LOVELAND, ASA, of Glastonbury, bound to Hosea Harris of Wethersfield until age 21, which will be on 21 Mar. 1767, to learn the trade of cordwainer.

IND. DATE: 19 Nov. 1763   CSL-005

LOVELAND, ELIJAH, ran away from Joseph Carver of Bolton. Elijah is age 17, has light hair, blue eyes (downward look), speaks slow, and of thick build. Knows shoemaker trade.

NEWSPAPER DATED: 18 Jun. 1798   CTC-001

LOVELAND, FREDERICK R., of East Hartford, born 15 Oct. 1861, child of Rollin Loveland, bound to Case Lockwood and Brainard Company of Hartford until age 21 to learn the trade of job compositor.

IND. DATE: 26 Jan. 1880   CHS-001

LOVELAND, JAMES MONROE, of East Hartford, born 13JUN1858, child of Rollin Loveland, bound to Case Lockwood & Brainard Company of Hartford until age 21 to learn the trade of job compositor.

IND. DATE: 07 Feb. 1876   CHS-001

LOVELAND, TIMOTHY, ran away from Charles Andrus, Jr. of Glastonbury. Timothy is age 20, 5' 8" tall, has long, brown hair, and light eyes. Trained as shoemaker. Reward 3 shillings.

NEWSPAPER DATED: 15 Feb. 1785   CTC-001

LOVELAND, WILLIAM HENRY, of Bolton, bound to David Sperry of Bolton until age 21, which will be on 06 Jul. 1852, to learn the trade of agriculture.

IND. DATE: 28 Oct. 1844   CSL-011

LUEDTKE, ANNIE - child of Timothy and Diane Luedtke of Simsbury, bound to Susan Marcus of Somerville, Massachusetts until age 18, which will be on 28 Jul. 1896 to learn the trade of servant.

IND. DATE: 30 Sep. 1886   APR-001

LYMAN, GAD, of Bolton, child of ( )eams Lyman, bound to Samuel Lyman of Bolton until age 21 to learn the trade of shoemaking and tanning.

IND. DATE: 14 Feb. 1799   CSL-011

LYMAN, POLLY, aged 8 on 15 Oct. 1791, child of Jabez Lyman, bound to Abner Clark of Lebanon until age 18.

IND. DATE: 27 Feb. 1792   CSL-004

LYMAN, POLLY, aged 13 on 15 Oct. 1796, bound to Ezekiel Wickwire of Lebanon until age 18.

IND. DATE: 27 Nov. 1797   CSL-004

MC CARTY, DAVID, aged about 12 in August 1808, bound to Dan Marsh Jr. of Lebanon until age 21 to learn the trade of farming. David is permitted to live with such mechanic as he chooses for the last 3 years of his service.

IND. DATE: 02 Dec. 1808   CSL-004

MC CARTY, JAMES, under 4 years old, child of John McCarty and wife Olive, bound to Joseph Pellett Jr.

IND. DATE: 20 Nov. 1780   CTH-001

MC CARTY, LOVISA, aged about 5 on August 14th last, bound to Elisha Bogue of Colchester until age 18.

IND. DATE: 20 Jan. 1800   CSL-004

MC CARTY, WILLIAM, child of John McCarty, bound to Jabez Green.

IND. DATE: 20 Jun. 1783   CTH-001

MC DONOUGH, ANN - Letter undated - "Sir - As soon as convenient I should like to have Mary bound to me as I think it probable her uncle may be after her this summer - her grandmother is in town, but I presume has no right to interfere as she has done nothing for the child." Signed Ann McDonough, Middletown.

RECORD: (Undated)   MHS-001

MC EVEN, JAMES, ran away from James Morgan of New Milford. James McEven is age 20, 5' 5" tall, is slender with round face. Trained as shoemaker. Reward $2.

NEWSPAPER DATED: 06 Jan. 1777   CTC-001

MC FALL, BILLE, of Wethersfield, child of Dinah Stoddard dec., bound to Luther Latimer of Wethersfield until age 21, which will be on 17 Apr. 1807, to learn the trade of farming.

IND. DATED: 10 Aug. 1789   CSL-005

MC INTYRE, JOHN, of Hartford, born 16 Nov. 1863, child of Hugh McIntyre, bound to Case Lockwood & Brainard Co. of Hartford until age 21, which will be on 16 Nov. 1884, to learn the trade of paper ruler.

IND. DATE: 10 Jan. 1881   CHS-001

MC KEE, FRANCIS, ran away from Elijah Boardman of Wethersfield. Francis is age 20, and has light complextion. By trade he is a house joiner. Reward $1.00.

NEWSPAPER DATED: 10 Jan. 1791   CTC-001

MC KUE, JAMES, lately from Ireland, ran away from Thomas Seymour of Hartford. James is a short, thick fellow with brown hair and blue eyes. Reward $5.

NEWSPAPER DATED: 15 May 1775   CTC-001

MC KEE, JOHN B., child of Agnes M. McKee, bound to Case Lockwood & Brainard Co. of Hartford until age 21, which will be on 08 Aug. 1873, to learn the trade of compositor.

IND. DATE: 05 Sep. 1870   CHS-001

MC NEAL, JOHN - Petition of Samuel Belden of Norwalk. Belden apprehended McNeal who escaped to Long Island for stealing goods valued at 100 pounds and court awarded him McNeal's service for 7 years to work out cost. Then McNeal ran off. Belden wants to be awarded costs.

RECORD DATED: May 1737   CSL-GA-014

MABERRY, POLLY, of Mansfield, aged between 14 & 15 years, bound to Capt. Samuel Southworth of Mansfield until age 18, which will be on 28 Dec. 1815, to learn the trade of housewifery.

IND. DATED: 14 May 1812   CSL-001

MACOMBER, CHARLES A., aged about 16 on 09 May 1874, child of Mrs. E. P. Macomber, bound to Case Lockwood & Brainard Co. of Hartford until age 21, which will be on 09 Apr. 1879, to learn the trade of compositor.

IND. DATE: 09 Apr. 1874   CHS-001

MAGG(OS), PATRICK, of New London, child of Elenor Magg(os), bound to Joshua Beckwith of Lyme for term of 13 years.

IND. DATE: 09 Jan. 1764   CSL-010

MAYNOR, ASA, of Groton - Letter to William Avery of Groton - instructions to deliver to Benjamin Brewster, attorney to Ebenezer Witter of Groton, the indenture of Asa Maynor.

RECORD DATED: 19 Apr. 1773   ICR-006

MAINER, NAHAM, of Groton, child of Mary Mainer, widow of Zachariah, bound to Ichabod Downing of Windham to learn trade of servant.

IND. DATE: 18 Oct. 1745(6)   CSL-017M

MAINARD, SALLY, of Tolland, illegitimate daughter of Ladema Mainard, bound to Jessey Eaton of Tolland until age 18, which will be on 11 Jan. 1835, to learn the trade of servant.

IND. DATE: 01 Sep. 1823   CSL-003

MALONE, WILLIAM, of Middletown, child of Michael Malone dec., bound to Luther Ford of Hebron until age 21, which will be on 15 May 1818, to learn the trade of farming.

IND. DATE: 28 Jun. 1813   MHS-001

MANAHAN, THOMAS, Irish boy, ran away from Tierbout & O'Brien (printing office in New Haven). Thomas is 5' 4" tall, has sandy hair, surley, down looking gaze, thick build, pitted from smallpox, and usually found quarreling as he is fond of strong drink.

NEWSPAPER DATED: 31 Aug. 1795   CTC-001

MARKHAM, ASA, ran away from Barzillai Markham of Enfield. Asa is age 16, 5' 4" tall, has dark brown hair, and light blue eyes. Reward six pence.

NEWSPAPER DATED: 28 Apr. 1788   CTC-001

MARKS, BILDAD, ran away from David Buckley of Berlin. Bildad is age 15 and has dark complextion. Reward 3 coppers.

NEWSPAPER DATED: 29 Oct. 1792   CTC-001

MARKS, BELDAD - Bond of Abisha Marks to release his son Beldad from indenture to David Beckley before time is up. States Beldad was born 02 Sep. 1777 and home is in Painted Pact in New York.

RECORD DATED: (undated)   CSL-005

MARSHALL, JOSEPH, of Windsor - At Inferior Court of Windsor, 15 July 174(2). Joseph Marshall brought before court on complaint of Elijah Yeomans of Tolland. On the 25th day of June, Joseph Marshall was lawfully bound to Yeomans. On 29 June, Joseph Marshall ran away from master.

RECORD DATED: 15 Jul. 174(2)   CHS-003

MARSHALL, LLOYD, of Middletown, child of Gad Marshall dec., bound to Joseph Coe, Jr. of Middletown until age 21, which will be on 05 Feb. 1794, to learn the trade of shoemaker.

IND. DATE: 21 Jan. 1782   MHS-001

MASKIL, THOMAS - Court found that Thomas Maskil is not legally bound to Captain Cooke as an apprentice.

RECORD DATED: 01 Sep. 1659   CSL-008

MASON, JONATHAN, of Wethersfield, aged 5 years, 4 months, so called child of Jonathan Mason, bound to Samuel Heel of Wethersfield until age 21 to learn the trade of weaving.

IND. DATE: 10 Mar. 1724/5   WHS-001

MATHER, JOHN, ran away from Nathaniel Hayden Jr. of Windsor. John is age 19, 5' 4" tall, has dark brown hair, and light complextion. Reward $1.

NEWSPAPER DATED: 01 May 1769   CTC-001

MATHEWS, MARY ANN, of Wethersfield, bound to Josiah Atwood of Wethersfield until age 18, which will be on 02 Jun. 1857, to learn the trade of servant.

IND. DATE: 17 Feb. 1851   CSL-033

MATTHEWSON, HARRIOT, of Ashford, bound to David Bolles of Ashford until age 18 to learn the trade of housewifery.

IND. DATE: 14 Mar. 1820   CSL-019M

MAXSON, WILLIAM, of New London, bound to Pierpont Bacon of Colchester for term of 15 years, 4 months, 12 days, at which time he will be 21, to learn the trade of husbandman.

IND. DATE: 26 Dec. 1770   CSL-010

MEACH, THOMAS, of Glastonbury, bound to John How of Glastonbury until age 21, which will be on 01 Mar. 1832, to learn the trade of husbandry.

IND. DATE: 07 Apr. 1818   GHS-001

MEAD, ( ), child of Abner Mead, bound to Eli Wilmot for term of 1 year to learn the trade of farming. Truman Kilborns' certificate dated 29 Jun. 1829-Bradleyville verified indenture.

IND. DATE: 31 Mar. 1828   LHS-003

MEIGS, HULDAH, of Middletown, child of Ezekiel Meigs dec., bound to Elisha Coe and wife Elisabeth of Middletown for term of 9 years to learn the trade of housewifery.

IND. DATE: 12 May 1788   MHS-001

MEIGS, RACHEL (JR.), of Middletown, child of Ezekiel Meigs dec., bound to Jonathan Thayer and wife Phebe of Middletown until age 18, which will be in April 1795, to learn the trade of housewifery.

IND. DATE: 11 Jun. 1787   MHS-001

MELONEY, NANCEY, of Middletown, bound to Samuel Cooper until age 18, which will be on 09 Jul. 1835, to learn the trade of housewifery.

IND. DATE: 07 Dec. 1829   MHS-001

MERRILL, TRUMAN, ran away from Samuel Stanley of West Hartford. Truman is age 18, 5' 10" tall, has short, light hair, and trained as clothier. Reward 1 shilling 6 pence.

NEWSPAPER DATED: 07 Sep. 1784   CTC-001

MERRIMAN, SAMUEL, ran away from Moses Smith of Farmington. Samuel is 5' 6" tall, has a round face, and knows shoemaker trade. Reward 20 shillings.

NEWSPAPER DATED: 30 Apr. 1770   CTC-001

MERRIT, EDWARD, ran away from John Merriam of Meriden. Edward is age 15, 5' 6" tall, has short, black hair tied behind, and dark eyes.

NEWSPAPER DATED: 10 Jun. 1783   CTC-001

MIDDLEWICK, CHARLES, native of Devonshire, England [now of city of New York] aged 16 years, 6 months, 5 days bound to Seneca Mosely of Glastonbury for term of 4 years, 5 months, 25 days (age 21) to learn the trade of shipmaster.

IND. DATE: 06 Sep. 1815   GHS-001

MILES, MARCUS, of New Haven, child of John Miles, Jr., bound to Ebenezar Bolles of Litchfield until age 21, which will be on 21 May 1792, to learn the trade of saddler.

IND. DATE: 17 May 1790   LHS-002

MILES, WILLIAM, of Middletown, bound to William Hamlin, Jr. of Middletown until age 21, which will be on 03 Jun. 1796, to learn the trade of husbandry.

IND. DATE: 05 Mar. 1792   MHS-001

MILLER, ELIZUR JR., of Glastonbury, child of Elizur Miller, bound to David Talcott, Jr. of Williston, Chittenden County, Vermont, until age 21, which will be on 14 May 1803, to learn the trade of shoemaking and tanning.

IND. DATE: 05 Oct. 1797   CSL-006

MILLER, HENRY, ran away from Camp Parmele. Henry is age 14. Reward one penny.

NEWSPAPER DATED: 29 Oct. 1792   CTC-001

MILLER, (HORACE), ran away from Thaddeus Taylor of Suffield. He is age 18, has dark brown hair, talkative and bold, light complextion, and walks with head sloping forward. Reward one copper.

NEWSPAPER DATED: 09 Jul. 1787   CTC-001

MILLER, JAMES - [fragment of a letter] - Mr. Owen - We wish you to deliver up the indenture to James Miller if his time is out that he may be enabled to get it fulfilled. We understand he was at first bound to Capt. James Fitch father in law to Col Mason and afterward [torn] the death of Mr. Fitch served Col. Mason [torn] now is entitled to the performance of the contract [torn] your delivering the indenture will entitle [torn] the fulfillment yr.

[Above note dated New London 23 May 1791 - Signature illegible]

RECORD DATED: 23 May 1791   CSL-010

MILLER, LEONARD, of Wethersfield, child of Ebenezer Miller, bound to William Williams of Wethersfield until age 21, which will be on 20 Jun. 1796, to learn the trade of cordwainer.

IND. DATE: 09 Dec. 1790   CSL-005

MILLERD, THOMAS - Thomas Millerd claimed Henry Woollcott Sr. wrongfully bound him as apprentice.

RECORD DATED: 02 Dec. 1652   CSL-008

MINER, HENERY, of Middlefield, Massachusetts, child of Hannah Miner, bound to Asa Brown of Washington, Massachusetts until age 21 to learn the trade of farming.

IND. DATE: 10 Mar. 1800   CSL-011

MINER, THEODE, bound to Capt. William Keeney of Waterford.

IND. DATE: 01 Nov. 1824   WTH-001

MIX, THOMAS, ran away from Asa Whitney of Salisbury. Thomas is age 16. Reward six pence.

NEWSPAPER DATED: 22 Aug. 1785   CTC-001

MOGER, STEPHEN, of New London, child of Sam Moger dec., bound to John Griffing of Lyme until age 21, which will be in Sept. 1775.

IND. DATE: 03 Jun. 1760   CSL-010

MONIGATI, JOHANN PHILIP, from Amsterdam, aged about 33 and wife Margaratha, age 28, were passengers on board ship Boyne. Benjamin Tallmadge of Litchfield paid shipmaster, Gilbert Floyd, $157 for couple to become servants to him. Couple agreed to serve an extra 6 months for every child that might be born during 3 year term of indenture.

IND. DATE: 26 Sep. 1797   LHS-004

MORAN, CHARLES (or Beckwith), bound to Jonathan Townsend of Hebron.

IND. DATE: 03 Feb. 1813   WTH-001

MORGAN, ABIGAIL, of Middletown, child of John Morgan, bound to John Ives of Wallingford until age 18, which will be on 24 Jun. 1792, to learn the trade of housewifery.

IND. DATE: 02 Sep. 1791   MHS-001

MORGAN, ASA, of Colchester, child of Lucretia Morgan, and with the approval of his guardian William Moseley of Glastonbury, binds himself to Hezekiah Beardslee of Wethersfield for term of one year to learn trade of shoemaker.

IND. DATE: 26 Aug. 1788   CSL-005

MORGAN, AVERY, ran away from Demick Morley of Glastonbury. Avery is age 20, has short hair and dark complextion.

NEWSPAPER DATED: 10 Aug. 1789   CTC-001

MORGON, EXPERIENCE, of Middletown, child of John Morgon, bound to Daniel Chattenton of Hamden until age 18, which will be on 02 Jun. 1794, to learn the trade of housewifery.

IND. DATE: 05 Sep. 1791   MHS-001

MORGAN, RICHARD, bound to Roswell Saltingstall of New London for term of 13 years, 4 months, 4 days, at which time he will be 21, to learn the trade of distilling of spirits.

IND. DATE: 05 Nov. 1770   CSL-010

MORGAN, THOMAS, ran away from Thadeus Granger of Suffield. Thomas is age 20 and has sandy hair. Reward 6 pence.

NEWSPAPER DATED: 06 Mar. 1797   CTC-001

MORGAN, ZADOCK, of Middletown, child of Simon Morgan, bound to Charles Francis of Middletown until age 14, which will be on 01 Apr. 1831, to learn the ways of economy.

IND. DATE: 06 Jun. 1825   MHS-001

MORLEY, JOHN, ran away from William Morley of Glastonbury. John is 5' 5" tall, has long, brown hair and a thin face.

NEWSPAPER DATED: 24 Nov. 1772   CTC-001

MORRISON, LINCOLN, of Thompsonville, born 12 Jan. 1867, child of James Morrison, bound to Case Lockwood & Brainard Co. of Hartford until age 21 to learn the trade of job pressman.

IND. DATE: 14 Dec. 1885   CHS-001

MOSIER, RICHARD CORT, of Lebanon, child of Richard S. Mosier, bound to Salmon Williams of Lebanon until age 21, which will be on 13 Mar. 1839, to learn the trade of blacksmith.

IND. DATE: 31 Mar. 1834   CSL-014

MOSELEY, ELIJAH JR., of Ashford, child of Elijah Moseley, bound to Calvin Morrey, Jr. of Union until age 21, which will be on 01 Oct. 1852, to learn the trade of farming.

IND. DATE: 10 Dec. 1840   CSL-019M

MOSELEY, SAMUEL, of Ashford, bound to Thomas W. Delphey of Willington until age 21 to learn the trade of farming.

IND. DATE: 18 Sep. 1841   CSL-019M

MOWRY, CLARISSA, bound to Warren Fitch of Tolland for term of 9 years, at which time she will be 18, to learn trade of servant. [indenture is unfinished and unsigned]

IND. DATE: 07 Nov. 1831   CSL-003

MOWRY, JOHN, of Tolland, bound to Levi Drake until age 21, which will be on 19 Jul. 1847, to learn the trade of farming.

IND. DATE: 01 Jan. 1838   CSL-003

MULLENDIRNE, JONAS, of New London, child of Mary Mullendirne dec., bound to Jonathan Star of Norwich for term of 15 years from 20th of Jan. last, at which time he will be age 21, to learn the trade of husbandry.

IND. DATE: 19 Mar. 1764   CSL-010

MULLENDIRNE, MARY, of New London, child of Jonas Mullendirne and Mary both dec., bound to Jonathan Star of Norwich for term of 14 years last day April instant, at which time she will be age 18, to learn the trade of housewifery.

IND. DATE: 02 Apr. 1764   CSL-010

MURPHY, (unnamed) - Letter: Male bastard child born 10 Jul. 1857 was abandoned in a boarding house in Unionville by his mother, Catherine Murphy, a foreigner. Child was 9 days old at time of mother's disappearance. Unnamed child was bound to Chapman S. Winchell of Canton to be named by him. Child will serve Winchell until age 21, which will be until 10 Jul. 1878.

IND. DATE: 24 Oct. 1857   CSL-007

MYGATE, THOMAS, of Wethersfield, child of Austin Mygate dec., bound to Daniel Deming 2nd of Wethersfield until age 21, which will be on 06 Jun. 1786, to learn the trade of cordwainer and tanner. Indenture made with the approval of his guardian Theodore Bukley of Wethersfield.

IND. DATE: 25 Feb. 1780   CSL-005

NELLIGAN, MICHAEL, age 16 years, 9 months, 12 days, bound to Sylester Lusk of Enfield for term of 4 years, 2 months, 18 days, to learn the trade of farming. Indenture made with the consent of the Managers of the Society for the Reformation of Juvenile Delinquents of New York.

IND. DATE: 20 Sep. 1838   CHS-004

NEWCOMB, OSCAR, age 7 on 31 March last, bound to Capt. Eliphalet Murdock of Windham until age 21 to learn the trade of husbandry.

IND. DATE: 06 Jul. 1795   CSL-004

NEWELL, NORMAN, ran away from Nehemiah Street of Farmington. Norman is age 14, has light complextion and brown hair. Reward 6 shillings.

NEWSPAPER DATED: 15 Mar. 1774   CTC-001

NOLTE, CHRISTIAN, son of William Nolte and Dorenda Bolin of Burlington, born 09 Jan. 1895, bound to Kathy Rogers of Windsor until 09 Jan. 1920 to learn the trade of husbandry.

IND. DATE: 07 Jul. 1918   APR-001

NORTON, ASA, of Suffield, child of John Norton, bound to Dr. Andrew Graham of Woodbury for term of 2 years (renegotiable to 3 years) to learn the trade of physicking. [Indenture was renewed to 3 years]

IND. DATE: 07 Apr. 1757   KML-001

NORTON, AUGUSTUS, of Farmington, bound to Edward Tillotson of Farmington until age 21, which will be on 01 Jun. 1842, to learn the trade of farming.

IND. DATE: 28 Aug. 1829   CSL-007

NORTON, HALSEY, of Middletown, aged about 6 on 13 Jul. last, child of Thomas Norton, bound to Nathaniel Cole of Berlin until age 21 to learn the trade of husbandry.

IND. DATE: 11 Jan. 1790   MHS-001

NORTEN, HANNAH, of Middletown, child of Aaron Norten, bound to Jehoshaphat Starr of Middletown until age 18, which will be on 20 Feb. 1812, to learn the trade of housewifery.

IND. DATE: 13 Jan. 1800   MHS-001

NORTON, WILLIAM, of Middletown, child of Jeremiah Norton dec., bound to Thomas Hall of Middletown until age 21, which will be on 11 Nov. 1830, to learn the trade of shoemaker.

IND. DATE: 23 Feb. 1824   MHS-001

OBED, JAMES, of Wethersfield, child of Hazard Obed, bound to Elisha Wolcott of Wethersfield until age 21, which will be on 25 Nov. 1833, to learn the trade of husbandry.

IND. DATE: 25 Feb. 1822   CSL-033

ORMSBY, (unnamed), bound to Gershom Hall.

IND. DATE: 15 Sep. 1777   CTH-001

ORMSBY, JOHN, child of Caleb Ormsby and wife Dorcas, bound to Lieut. Joseph Farnam.

IND. DATE: 21 Jul. 1770   CTH-001

ORMSBY, PHEBE, child of Caleb Ormsby and wife Dorcas, bound to Moses Hagget Jr.

IND. DATE: 07 Jun. 1770   CTH-001

ORR, THOMAS, of Glastonbury, bound to Jonathan Talcott of Glastonbury until age 21, which will be on 19 Jan. 1800, to learn the trade of husbandry.

IND. DATE: 14 Mar. 1785   GHS-001

OTICE, WILLIAM, of New London, bound to Amos Avery of Groton for term of 7 years, 9 months, at which time he will be age 21, to learn the trade of shoemaker.

IND. DATE: 04 Jun. 1770   CSL-010

OWEN, ELIJAH, of Windsor, aged about 17, child of Elijah Owen dec., and with the approval of his guardian Jn Isaac Owen, does bind himself to Nathaniel Hayden of Windsor for term of 3 years, 4 months, 26 days to learn the trade of shoemaker and tanner.

IND. DATE: 15 May 1756   CHS-005

OWEN, GIDEON, ran away from Daniel Beebe of Canaan. Gideon is age 15, has light hair, light complexion, and "guilty fox eye".

NEWSPAPER DATED: 01 Aug. 1780   CTC-001

PACKER, SAMUEL, of Groton, child of James Packer, bound to James Rogers of New London for term of 1 year, 5 months, to learn the trade of cooper and navigation.

IND. DATE: 29 Jan. 1745   CSL-010

PAC(T), JAMES, of New London, aged about 13, bound to Nathaniel Richards of New London until age 21 to learn the trade of navigation.

IND. DATE: 29 Mar. 1779   CSL-010

PALMER, ABRAHAM, of New London, bound to John Wickwi(n)e of New London until age 14.

IND. DATE: 04 Jul. 1768   CSL-010

PALMER, CHARLES A., of Litchfield, child of Simeon Palmer, bound to Jacob Turner of Litchfield for term of 8 months. [Indenture unsigned]

IND. DATE: 27 Mar. 1832   LHS-005

PAMHAM, JOSEPH, of Mansfield, bound to Samuel Flint of Windham for 4 1/2 months to satisfy debt.

IND. DATE: 17 Mar. 1761   CHS-003

PARKE, ASA, ran away from Nathaniel Satterlee of Plainfield. Asa is age 19, 5' 8" tall, and is well built. Reward $5.

NEWSPAPER DATED: 07 Jun. 1774   CTC-001

PARKER, ELIJAH, of Coventry, bound to James Parker of Coventry for term of 1 year to satisfy debt.

IND. DATE: 13 Feb. 1755   CHS-003

PARKER, ELISHA, of Mansfield, bound to Stephen Freeman of Mansfield for term of 4 1/2 years to satisfy debt.

IND. DATE: 13 Apr. 1758   CHS-003

PARKER, ZACHARIAH, of Mansfield, bound to Hezekiah Storrs of Mansfield until 01 Aug. 1756 to satisfy debt.

IND. DATE: 12 Mar. 1755   CHS-003

PARKS, EBENEZAR, ran away from Thomas Stedman, Jr. of Windham. Ebenezar is age 19, fat fellow with one eye lid 1/2 white and 1/2 colored.

NEWSPAPER DATED: 20 Mar. 1769   CTC-001

PARRISH, PATIENCE, child of Lydia Parrish, bound to Joel Dodge.

IND. DATE: 10 Apr. 1769   CTH-001

PARSONS, DAVID, of New London, aged about 10, bound to Phillip Morgan of New London until age 21 to learn the trade of husbandry.

IND. DATE: 05 May 1778   CSL-010

PEACHGOOD, EDWARD, of Wethersfield, child of Hannah Peachgood, bound to Aclee Riley of Wethersfield until age 21, which will be on 03 May 1800, to learn the trade of navigation.

IND. DATE: ( ) Sep. 1781   CSL-005

PEASE, ANTHONY, ran away from Ephraim Pease of Enfield. Anthony is age 15, 5' tall, has light hair and light complextion. Reward $2.

NEWSPAPER DATED: 18 Jul. 1796   CTC-001

PEASE, DAVID, ran away from Reuben Skinner of Bolton. David is age 19.

NEWSPAPER DATED: 14 Jun. 1790   CTC-001

PEASE, HAPSY, of Glastonbury, aged about 16 the 15 Apr. last, child of Peter Pease, bound to John Miller of Glastonbury until age 18, term of 1 year, to learn trade of servant.

IND. DATE: 19 Aug. 1791   CSL-006

PEASE, PETER JR., of Glastonbury, child of Peter Pease and wife Sarah, bound to Elizur Hale, Jr. of Glastonbury until age 21 to learn the trade of husbandry. Sarah Pease is now Sarah Smythers, wife of William Smythers of Glastonbury.

IND. DATE: 03 Mar. 1779   CSL-006

PELTON, HULDAY, of Groton, child of Ruben Pelton, bound to Joseph Morgan, Jr. and wife Prudence until age 18.

IND. DATE: 04 Jan. 1703   ICR-003

PELTON, JOSEPH, of Groton, child of Rubin Pelton, bound to Paul Pelton of Groton until age 21.

IND. DATE: 16 Mar. 1763   ICR-003

PERKINS, GEORGE E., born 06 Sep. 1860, child of G. S. Perkins, bound to Case Lockwood & Brainard Co. of Hartford until age 21 to learn the trade of bookbinder and forwarder.

IND. DATE: 19 Sep. 1877   CHS-001

PETERS, SAMUEL - Letter: "To Selectmen of Middletown: My son Samuel Peters is now living with Joel (Foote) Esq. of Marlborough and I wish to have him bound out to him until he arrives to the age of 21. The Mr. Foote doing by the boy as is customary and learn him a trade." Signed by Fortune Russell and Jane Russell.

IND. DATE: 28 Mar. 1826   MHS-001

PETERS, SELSON, of Middletown bound to Horace Skinner of Middletown until age 21, which will be on 02 Jan. 1844, to learn the trade of farming.

IND. DATE: 07 Jan. 1833   MHS-001

PHELPS, ASAHEL, of Bolton, child of Asahel Phelps and Martha Brunson bound to Cone Andrews of Ellington until age 21 to learn the trade of carpenter or joiner.

IND. DATE: 07 Jan. 1799   CSL-011

PHILLIPS, NORMAN, of Mansfield, bound to Barzillan Swift of Mansfield until age 21, which will be on 17 Jun. 1824, to learn the trade of husbandry.

IND. DATE: 07 Mar. 1808   CSL-001

PHILLIPS, SAMUEL, ran away from Joab Griswold of Windsor. Samuel is age 13, has short, dark brown hair, and of middling size. Took with him small yellow dog. Reward 3 shillings 2 p - return of dog only - 3 shillings.

NEWSPAPER DATED: 19 Sep. 1796   CTC-001

PICKET, RUFUS, of Danbury, child of Ebenezer Picket, bound to Friend Starr of Danbury for term of 1 year, 11 months, 4 days to learn the trade of shoemaking.

IND. DATE: 27 Aug. 1803   LHS-006

PIERCE, EPHRAIM JR., ran away from Charles Bingham of Ellington. Ephraim is age 19. Reward 2 pence.

NEWSPAPER DATED: 07 Sep. 1795   CTC-001

PIERCE, THOMAS, ran away from Ebenezar Faxon of Hartford. Thomas is age 21, thick, stout fellow. Reward $3.

NEWSPAPER DATED: 20 Jul. 1773   CTC-001

PIKE, LUCE, of Norwich, child of Widow Mary Pike, bound to John Birchard and wife Mary of Norwich until age 17 to learn the trade of servant.

IND. DATE: 07 Jul. 1748   CSL-017M

PILLION, WILLIAM, born 07 Feb. 1867, child of Kieran Pillion, bound to Case Lockwood & Brainard Co. of Hartford until age 21 1/2, which will be on 07 Aug. 1888, to learn the trade of book compositor.

IND. DATE: 09 Mar. 1885   CHS-001

POLLY, HANNAH, bound to Asahel Williams and wife Esther of Lebanon until age 18, which will be on 01 Mar. 1798.

IND. DATE: 22 Mar. 1790   CSL-004

POLLY, ROBERT, aged about 13 on 22 April next, bound to Asa Torrey of Lebanon until age 21 to learn the trade of blacksmithing.

IND. DATE: 17 Feb. 1790   CSL-004

PORTER, CHARLES S., aged about 17 on 03 Jun. 1870, and with the approval of guardian Nathaniel Root, Jr., bound to Case Lockwood & Brainard Co. of Hartford until age 21, which will be on 09 May 1874, to learn the trade of compositor.

IND. DATE: 09 May 1871   CHS-001

PORTER, LEVI, of Farmington, child of Benjamin Porter dec., and with the approval of guardian Robert Porter, bound to Israel Curtis of Farmington until age 21 to learn the trade of blacksmith.

IND. DATE: 04 Feb. 1761   STL-002

PORTER, ROBERT, of Litchfield, child of John Porter of Woodbury, bound to Rev. Joseph Bellamy of Woodbury for a term of 11 years, 20 days to learn the trade of servant.

IND. DATE: 10 Dec. 1773   CHS-011

POTTER, AUGUSTUS, of Glastonbury, bound to James Alger of Glastonbury until age 21 to learn the trade of husbandry.

IND. DATE: (undated)   GHS-001

POTTER, JOHN, aged about 13 years, 5 months, bound to Sylvestor Lusk of Enfield for term of 6 years, 6 months to learn the trade of farming. Indenture made with the consent of the Managers of Society for the Reformation of Juvenile Delinquents of New York.

IND. DATE: 01 Oct. 1833   CHS-004

POWERS, MICHAEL, child of Widow Phebe Powers, bound to David Ames of Montville.

IND. DATE: 15 Mar. 1813   WTH-001

PRENTICE, (unnamed), son of Widow Prentice bound to Stephen Spalding.

IND. DATE: 13 Mar. 1775   CTH-001

PRATT, GEORGE - Indenture binding George Pratt as physician and surgeon to poor of Windsor for $9 for period of 01 Mar. 1812 to 28 Feb. 1813.

IND. DATE: 01 Mar. 1812   WNH-002

PRENTICE, DEMIS, bound to Deacon Jonas Bond.

IND. DATE: 01 Mar. 1779   CTH-001

PRESTON, STEPHEN - Letter dated New London: "Sir please to deliver to Stephen Preston the bairer the indenture of said Stephen to Jeremiah Ross - lodged in your office - am" [illegible]. Signed by Joseph Harris, David Wright, and George Williams - Selectmen; and Mr. Jn Owen Town Clerk.

RECORD DATED: 07 Nov. 1787   CSL-010

PRINCE, LENT (bastard), of Middletown bound to Samuel Confield of Middletown until age 21, which will be on 12 Jul. 1813, to learn the trade of husbandry.

IND. DATE: 09 Feb. 1795   MHS-001

PRIOR, WILLIAM HARVEY, of Middletown, bound to Townsend Way of Middletown until age 21, which will be on 01 Oct. 1851, to learn the trade of paper staining.

IND. DATE: 03 May 1841   MHS-001

PRUDDEN, JOSEPH, of Wethersfield, bound to Henry Wells of Hartford until age 21, which will be on 16 Jun. 1830, to learn the trade of boot and shoemaking.

IND. DATE: 29 Oct. 1827   CSL-033

PRUDDEN, MARY, of Wethersfield, bound to James L. Reynolds of Enfield until age 18, which will be on 03 Mar. 1818, to learn the trade of housewifery.

IND. DATE: 11 Mar. 1816   CSL-005

QUIMLY, THOMAS, of New London, bound to John Hempsted of New London for a term of 9 years, 14 days, at which time he will be 21, to learn the trade of husbandry.

IND. DATE: 01 Jun. 1767   CSL-010

QUINLEY, JAMES, of Middletown, child of David C. Quinley, bound to Aaron Richards of Wethersfield until age 16, which will be on 01 Jan. 1838 to learn the trade of farming.

IND. DATE: 06 Feb. 1832   MHS-001

RAND, DANIEL, 2nd, of Middletown bound to Miles Merwin, Jr. of Durham until age 16, which will be on 16 Sep. 1836, to learn the trade of husbandry.

IND. DATE: 07 Dec. 1829   MHS-001

RAND, WILLIAM, of Middletown, child of William Rand, bound to Timothy Stone of Durham until age 21, which will be on 04 Dec. 1826, to learn the trade of husbandry.

IND. DATE: 20 Dec. 1819   MHS-001

RAYMOND, JOSIAH Jr. - Petition of Hannah Raymond, of Ridgefield, showing that her husband Josiah absconded and wants to bind out her son.

IND. DATE: May 1797   CSL-GA-05

RAYNSFORD, NATHAN, child of Jonathan Raynsford, bound to Moses Goodale for term of 2 1/2 years.

IND. DATE: 05 Jun. 1778   CTH-001

RANDALL, JOSEPH - "Run-away from the subscriber the 10th of May one Joseph Randall, a tall trim built fellow; had on when he went away a blue coat, velvet waistcoat and breeches, mixed coloured stockings, and wore away two felt hats; he rode away a black horse and led a ( ) horse; he is supposed to be lurking in the south part of Scantick after a strumpet that he has spent the most of his time with for three years past. Whoever will take up said Randall and return him to me shall have three coppers reward; but whoever will take the trouble to keep him away shall have Ten Dollars and all necessary charges paid, by me." Susanna Randall.

NEWSPAPER DATED: 16 May 1788   CTC-001

RANNEY, SETH, ran away from Amos Sage of Middletown. Seth is age 18, 5' 6" tall. Reward $50.

NEWSPAPER DATED: 16 Nov. 1779   CTC-001

READ, LAWRENCE, of Mansfield, is bound out by his master, Aaron Hovey of Mansfield, to Jasper Woodworth of Coventry until age 21, which will be on 15 Aug. 1813, to learn the trade of husbandry.

IND. DATE: 26 Mar. 1811   CSL-037M

RECO(R), ELZA, inmate of almshouse in Farmington, child of Lucinda Hart dec., bound to Levi Whitney of Canton until age 21, which will be on 21 May 1860, to learn the trade of housewifery.

IND. DATE: 20 Sep. 1848   CSL-007

REDFIN, JAMES, of New London, child of William Redfin, bound to Hugh Roberts for term of 5 years to learn the trade of tanner.

IND. DATE: 01 Apr. 1662   NLT-002

RICH, LEVI, so called bastard child of Eunice Thomas, born 16 Jul. 1787, bound to Capt. Elias Bliss of Lebanon until age 21 to learn the trade of husbandry.

IND. DATE: 09 Dec. 1793   CSL-004

RICHARDS, ALLEN, bound to Elias P. Haynes until age 21 to learn the trade of house carpentry and joining.

IND. DATE: 03 Oct. 1833   WTH-001

RICHARDS, GILES, ran away from Joseph Hopkins of Waterbury. Giles is age 19, 5' 9" tall, has light brown hair, light eyes, fair complection, well educated, and trained as goldsmith. Reward $10.

NEWSPAPER DATED: 17 Nov. 1772   CTC-001

RICHARDS, STEPHEN, of New London, age 9, bound to Jedidiah Chapill of New London until age 21 to learn the trade of husbandry.

IND. DATE: 03 May 1779   CSL-010

RILEY, SYLVESTER W., of Wethersfield, child of Eunice Riley, bound to Justis Riley and wife Eunice Fortune to learn the trade of tanning and currying.

IND. DATE: 29 Nov. 1813   CSL-005

RISLEY, JOSHUA, ran away from Charles Reynolds of East Hartford. Joshua is age 18, 5' 6" tall, has black hair and black eyes. By trade blacksmith. Reward 3 pence half penny.

NEWSPAPER DATED: 06 Sep. 1790   CTC-001

RIXFORD, GEORGE, of Hebron, child of Luther Rixford, bound to James Aspenwall of Canterbury until 01 Sep. 1836.

IND. DATE: 26 Nov. 1827   CSL-038M

ROBBENS, CALEB, ran away from Saul Alvord Jr. of Bolton. Caleb is age 19 and has dark complection.

NEWSPAPER DATED: 27 May 1793   CTC-001

ROBBINS, JONATHAN, JR., of Wethersfield, child of Jonathan Robbins, bound to Elisha Wells of Wethersfield until age 21, which will be on 27 Nov. 1792, to learn the trade of shoemaker.

IND. DATE: 15 Dec. 1787   CSL-005

ROBBINS, ROCKCENERY, daughter of Eunice Robbins of Bolton, bound to Caleb Robbins of Berlin. (Indenture is a fragment)

IND. DATE: 31 Oct. 1797   CSL-011

ROBINS, SARAH, aged about 6 on 6 September next, child of Thomas Robins of Farmington, bound to John Hart of Farmington until age 18 to learn the trade of housewifery.

IND. DATE: 30 May 1754   STL-002-A

ROBBINS, WINTHROP, of Wethersfield, bound to Justus Griswold of Wethersfield until age 21, which will be on 11 May 1827, to learn the trade of clothier and dyer.

IND. DATE: 08 Apr. 1816   CSL-005

ROBERTS, JOHN, of Tolland, child of John Roberts dec., bound to Ichabod Hinckley of Tolland until age 21 to learn the trade of husbandry.

IND. DATE: 27 Jun. 1781   CSL-003

ROBERTS, JONATHAN, of Tolland, child of John Roberts dec., bound to Capt. James Chamberling of East Windsor until age 21 to learn the trade of husbandry.

IND. DATE: 17 Sep. 1782   CSL-003

ROBARDS, SETH, ran away from Thomas Newhall of Hartford. Seth is age 19, 5' 9" tall, has long, brown hair, and swarthy complexion. Reward $3.00.

NEWSPAPER DATED: 12 Oct. 1767   CTC-001

ROBERTS, SYLVESTOR, ran away from Charles Reynolds of East Hartford. Sylvestor is age 19, 5' 10" tall, has long, brown hair, grey eyes, light complextion, and is thin. By trade blacksmith.

NEWSPAPER DATED: 06 Sep. 1790   CTC-001

ROBINSON, ALLEN of Farmington bound to Asa Andrus of Farmington until age 21, which will be on 02 Jan. 1822, to learn the trade of japaning tin work.

IND. DATE: 23 May 1816   CSL-007

ROBINSON, AUGUSTUS, of Farmington, child of Amos Robinson, bound to Pomeroy Strong of Farmington until age 21, which will be on 03 Dec. 1826, to learn the trade of shoemaker/tanner. [Word "September" crossed out on indenture]

IND. DATE: 31 Oct. 1818   CSL-007

ROBINSON, BENJAMIN, of Killingly, bound to David Waters of Killingly for 2 years to satisfy debt.

IND. DATE: 11 Apr. 1755   CHS-003

ROBINSON, GEORGE, of Farmington, bound to Augustus Bodwell of Farmington until age 21, which will be on 05 Aug. 1824, to learn the trade of harness maker.

IND. DATE: 27 Apr. 1816   CSL-007

ROBINSON, GEORGE, of Farmington, bound to Asabel Woodruff of Farmington until age 21, which will be on 05 Apr. 1824, to learn the trade of sadler and harness maker.

IND. DATE: 01 Oct. 1821   CSL-007

ROBINSON, ISAAC, bound to Joseph Woodward of Windham for term of 5 years to satisfy debt.

IND. DATE: 22 Apr. 1755   CHS-003

ROBINSON, JAMES, ran away from Nicholas Brown of Hartford. James is age 18, 5' 4" tall, has brown hair and dark complextion. Reward 10 shillings.

NEWSPAPER DATED: 30 Apr. 1770   CTC-001

ROBINSON, JULIUS, of Farmington, child of Allen Robinson, bound to Erastus Bunnell of Southington until age 16, which will be on 01 Oct. 1860.

IND. DATE: 14 Apr. 1854   CSL-007

ROBINSON, OBEDIAH, of Killingly, bound to Nicholas Parker of Killingly for 4 months to satisfy debt.

IND. DATE: 02 Mar. 1761   CHS-003

ROBINSON, RICHARD, of Middletown, child of James Robinson, bound to John Rogers of Middletown until age 21, which will be on 05 Feb. 1807, to learn the trade of cooper.

IND. DATE: 11 May 1801   MHS-001

ROBINSON, WILLIAM, ran away from Demmick Morley of Glastonbury. William is age 17, 5' 8" tall, has dark hair, dark eyes, ruddy complection, and light skin.

NEWSPAPER DATED: 25 Jan. 1785   CTC-001

ROCK, DAVID, ran away from Harb Wyles of Bolton. David is age 17 and has light complextion. Reward $4.

NEWSPAPER DATED: 27 May 1799   CTC-001

ROGERS, CHARITY, of New London, bound to John Harris the third and wife Hannah of New London for term of 6 years, 1 month, 28 days, at which time she will be 18, to learn the trade of weaver.

IND. DATE: 15 Jan. 1771   CSL-010

ROGERS, JAMES A., of Hartford, born 24 Sep. 1864, child of James E. Rogers bound to Case Lockwood & Brainard Co. of Hartford until 24 Sep. 1884 to learn the trade of job compositor.

IND. DATE: 21 Nov. 1881   CHS-001

ROGERS, MARY ANN, of Wethersfield bound to Elisha Dodd of Hartford until age 18 to learn the trade of servant.

IND. DATE: 06 Sep. 1831   •   CSL-033

ROOT, (ARNIE), of Farmington, child of Seth Root, bound to Miles Crampton of Farmington until age 16, which will be on 04 Jul. 1815, to learn the trade of husbandry.

IND. DATE: 08 Jun. 1810   CSL-007

ROOT, HENRY, of Farmington, child of Seth Root, bound to Mann(a) Orvice of Farmington until age 21, which will be on 04 Aug. 1817.

IND. DATE: 28 Mar. 1814   CSL-007

ROOT, NANCY L., of Farmington, bound to Silas Hoadley of Plymouth until age 18, which will be on 29 Jun. 1841, to learn the trade of housewifery.

IND. DATE: 01 Sep. 1835   CSL-007

ROOT, TIMOTHY, of Farmington, child of Timothy Root dec., with the consent of his guardian and father in law Rev. Samuel Newell, binds himself to Elijah Cowles of Farmington until age 21 to learn the trade of shoemaker/tanner.

IND. DATE: 26 Jun. 1760   STL-002

ROSE, GEORGE, of Middletown, bound to Edmund Hughes of Middletown until age 21, which will be on 07 Mar. 1832, to learn the trade of silversmith.

IND. DATE: 04 Jun. 1827   MHS-001

ROSE, MARY ANN, of Farmington, child of Naomi Rose, bound to Asa Francis of Hartford until age 18, which will be on 13 May 1816 to learn the trade of housewifery.

IND. DATE: 21 Mar. 1810   CSL-007

ROWLANDSON, PHINEHAS, of Wethersfield, child of Rana Rowlandson, bound to Zebulon Robbins of Wethersfield for term of one year.

IND. DATE: 28 May 1785   CSL-005

ROWLANDSON, SARAH, of Wethersfield, child of Wilson and wife Anna Rowlandson both dec., bound to Abel Morse and wife Mehetable of Wethersfield until age 18 to learn the trade of housewifery.

IND. DATE: 08 Oct. 1779   CSL-005

ROWLANDSON, SARAH, of Wethersfield, child of Wilson and wife Anne Rowlandson both dec., bound to Aaron Porter Jr. and wife Lou of Wethersfield until age 18 to learn the trade of spinning.

IND. DATE: 27 Feb. 1781   CSL-005

ROWLANDSON, WILLIAM ran away from Robert Wells of Wethersfield. William is age 20, of middling stature and has dark bushy hair and dark complection. Reward $6.

NEWSPAPER DATED: 09 Jun. 1794   CTC-001

ROYCE, ANDREW M., orphan of Andrew Royce dec. of Ellington, bound to Alonzo H. Piek of Ellington until age 21, which will be on 30 Aug. 1890, to learn the trade of farming.

IND. DATE: 24 Dec. 1877   CSL-031

ROYCE, HENRY, bound to Daniel Sessins of Mansfield until age 16, which will be on 22 Jun. 1833, to learn the trade of farming.

IND. DATE: 26 Sep. 1825   CSL-001

RUDE, BETSY ANN - [fragment] [left blank] contracted to keep Betsy Ann Rude until age 18, which will be on 23 Jul. 1827, for $30. [unsigned and unfinished indenture].

IND. DATE: 08 Mar. 1814   HBT-002

RUPEL, HARRY, of Glastonbury, bound to Reuben Curtice of Glastonbury until age 21, which will be on 01 Sep. 1833, to learn the trade of husbandry.

IND. DATE: 18 Sep. 1821   CSL-006

RUSSELL, ASHBEL, of Wethersfield, child of Arthur Russell, bound to Thomas Danforth of Wethersfield until age 21, which will be on 10 Jul. 1808, to learn the trade of tin plate work.

IND. DATE: 06 Apr. 1803   CSL-005

RUSSELL, GEORGE, of Wethersfield, child of Arthur Russell, bound to Abraham Jagger of Wethersfield until age 21, which will be on 01 Mar.1804, to learn the trade of cooper.

IND. DATE: 09 Dec. 1790   CSL-005

RUSSEL, JOSIAH, ran away from Ashbel Spencer of New Hartford. Josiah is age 18, short, with light hair. Reward 3 pence.

NEWSPAPER DATED: 11 Mar. 1793   CTC-001

RUSSELL, RICHARD, of Stafford County England, child of Ann Russell of Wednesbury County of Hartford, bound to Joseph Turner of Birmingham County of Warwick for term of 7 years to learn the trade of gun barrel filer.

IND. DATE: 10 May 1819   CHS-012

RUST, HEZEKIAH, ran away from Ebenezer Fletcher of Salisbury. Hezekiah is age 18, 5' 3" tall, has light brown hair cut bare on top of his head and brown complection. Reward $4.

NEWSPAPER DATED: 26 May 1766   CTC-001

SABIN, JOHN, ran away from Jazaniah Post of Tolland. John is age 17.

NEWSPAPER DATED: 30 May 1785   CTC-001

SACKETT, JOSEPH - Suit with William Worthington of Hartford over contract. Apprentice Joseph Sacket of Westfield and latters claim he was not taught to read and write.

RECORD DATED: 1709-1715   CSL-GA-015

SAGE, LUTHER, ran away from Joel Sexton of Simsbury. Luther is 5' tall and very thick set. Reward six pence.

NEWSPAPER DATED: 27 May 1793   CTC-001

SAMMON, HENRY - 17 Jun. 1653 - Servant to Mrs. Mary Chester of Wethersfield, was bound to her son, John Chester, of Wethersfield as apprentice for term of 5 years from 4th day August instant to learn trade of husbandry.

14 Feb. 1654 - Bound as servant to Mr. John Winthrop, Jr., of Pequod.

08 Apr. 1654 - John Chester of Wethersfield assigned Henry Sammon to Robert Griffin of Newport, Rhode Island, for term of one year and a half.

IND. DATES: 17 Jun. 1653 14 Feb. 1654 08 Apr. 1654   CSL-039M

SAUNDERS, JOSEPH, bound to Wilson Beckwith of East Haddam until age 16.

IND. DATE: 30 Mar. 1837   CSL-014

SAUNDERS, SAMUEL STEDMAN of Mansfield bound to Ebenezer Bosworth of Ashford until age 21, which will be on 23 Jan. 1833, to learn the trade of husbandry.

IND. DATE: 06 Dec. 1819   CSL-001

SAWYER, JACOB, of Middletown, child of Vina Sawyer, bound to Hosea Goodrich of Middletown until age 21, which will be on 23 Aug. 1817, to learn the trade of shoemaker.

IND. DATE: 09 Aug. 1802   MHS-001

SAYRE, PAUL, native of Long Island, ran away from James Tiley. Paul is age 19, 5' 7" tall, has short straight dark hair, light eyes, thick set, thick lips, flat nose, and face is pitted from small pox. Knows goldsmith trade. Reward $100 dollars continental money.

NEWSPAPER DATED: 25 Apr. 1780   CTC-001

SCIPION, THOMAS, of New London, bound to Simon Wolcot for term of 8 years, at which time he will be age 21.

IND. DATE: 12 Jan. 1778   CSL-010

SCOT, ASAHEL MORRIS, ran away from Ashbel King of Suffield. Asahel Scot is age 19, slim build, and light complection.

NEWSPAPER DATED: 05 Sep. 1791   CTC-001

SCOTT, LEMUEL, of Tolland, bound to Luther Eaton and Elmer Loomis of Tolland for term of 2 years from 14 Jan. 1834 to learn the trade of servant. [2 indentures - sum of $50 paid to Eaton and Loomis to take indenture from Henry and Joseph Straight].

IND. DATES: 22 Jan. 1834/14 Jan. 1836   CSL-003

SCOTT, SILAS, of Glastonbury, child of Joseph Scott, bound to David Taylor of Tioga County, Union, New York, until age 21, which will be on 11 Dec. 1812, to learn the trade of sadler.

IND. DATE: 16 Feb. 1802   CSL-006

SCOVIL, ARTHUR A. - Petition to General Assembly showing that he had moved from Yorkshire, England about 5 years ago and has leased land and set up a woolen business in said town. Wants tax exemption for his property and for himself and his apprentices and also exemption from military duty for himself, his son, and his apprentices.

RECORD DATED: 19 May 1802   CSL-GA-016

SCOVIL, WILLIAM WADSWORTH, with the consent of his guardian Phillip Capen, bound to Robert W. Chapman of East Haddam until age 21, which will be on 19 Jun. 1855, to learn trade of farming.

IND. DATE: 01 Jul. 1842   CSL-040M

SEARE, SILAS, native of Long Island, ran away from Elijah Hinsdale of New Britain. Silas is 5' 8" tall, age 19, and very thick build.

NEWSPAPER DATED: 14 Nov. 1780   CTC-001

SERKER, CHARLES, ran away from Simon Fobes, Jr. of Somers. Charles is by trade farmer. Reward 3 pence.

NEWSPAPER DATED: 02 Dec. 1793   CTC-001

SEYMOUR, DAVID, of New London, child of Thomas Seymour of Hartford, bound to David Gardiner of New London for term of 3 years, 6 months to learn the trade of traffick/trading/merchandise.

IND. DATE: 31 Dec. 1751   CSL-010

SEYMOUR, SAMUEL, age 16, bound by Capt. Alexander Catlin of Litchfield to Reuben Webster of Catskill Landing, New York, until age 21 to learn the trade of joiner.

IND. DATE: 26 Jan. 1797   LHS-007

SEXTON, BENJAMIN (formerly of Middletown, now of Chatham), with approval of his guardian John Shepard, Jr. of Chatham, binds himself to Elisa Buel of Colchester until age 21 to learn the trade of blacksmith.

IND. DATE: 07 May 1788   CSL-041M

SAXTON, ELEANOR, of Middletown, child of Knight Saxton, bound to Capt. Thompson Phillips and wife Abigail of Middletown until age 18 to learn the trade of housewifery.

IND. DATE: 09 Jul. 1787   MHS-001

SAXTON, THOMAS, of Middletown, child of Knight Saxton, bound to Capt. George Starr of Middletown until age 21 to learn the trade of rope maker.

IND. DATE: 19 Nov. 1787   MHS-001

SEXSTON, DANIEL - Apprentices Daniel Sexston, John Moses and Nathaniel Pond claim Nicholas Session attempted sodomy with them. Nicholas Session claims this is slander. Several witnesses including Joseph Phelps of Windsor testify to sodomy attempts. Nicholas is found guilty but does not receive prison sentence - court charges him 300 pounds and releases him on own recognizance.

RECORD DATED: May 1677   CSL-GA-017

SHACKMAPLE, ELISABETH, of New London, bound to Jabez Beebee of New London for term of 7 years, 9 months, 17 days, until age 18, to learn the trade of housewifery.

IND. DATE: 07 Dec. 1767   CSL-010

SHARRET, LUCRETIA, of New London, bound to James Cook Jr. and wife Sarah of Norwich for term of 4 years, 27 days, at which time she will be age 18, to learn the trade of housewifery.

IND. DATE: 01 Jun. 1767   CSL-010

SHEPARD, ANNA, of Farmington, child of Jonathan Shepard and wife both dec., bound to Thomas K. Brace of Hartford until age 18, which will be on 02 Nov. 1816, to learn the trade of housewifery.

IND. DATE: 09 Nov. 1812   CSL-007

SHEPARD, LOVINA, of Farmington, child of Jonathan Shepard, bound to Chauncy Gleason of Hartford until age 18, which will be on 11 Jun. 1815, to learn the trade of housewifery.

IND. DATE: 24 Jun. 1809   CSL-007

SIERS, ALANSON, of Glastonbury, bound to Elizur Tyron of Glastonbury until age 21, which will be on 01 May 1832, to learn the trade of husbandry.

IND. DATE: 24 Nov. 1817   GHS-001

SIFLAND, ZENAS, of Farmington, son of Martha Shelsy, bound to Charles Woodford of Farmington until age 21, which will be on 15 Nov. 1819, to learn the trade of husbandry.

IND. DATE: 16 Nov. 1812   CSL-007

SKINNER, CHARLES M., child of Charles A. Skinner, bound to Case Lockwood and Brainard Co. of Hartford until age 21, which will be on 15 Mar. 1873, to learn the trade of compositor.

IND. DATE: 16 Apr. 1869   CHS-001

SMEEDS, DAVID of Farmington, illegitimate son of Pat Clark, bound to Thomas Gleason until age 21, which will be on 06 Jul. 1828.

IND. DATE: 07 Jan. 1813   CSL-007

SMITH, BETSEY, child of Sally Strong, bound to John Tobey of Tolland until age 18, which will be on 11 Dec. 1844, to learn domestic female education.

IND. DATE: 07 Apr. 1829   CSL-003

SMITH, CHAUNCEY, of Farmington, bound to Ezekiel Cowles, Jr. of Farmington until age 21, which will be on 12 Feb. 1798, to learn the trade of shoemaker/tanner.

IND. DATE: 18 Nov. 1793   CSL-007

SMITH, CYRIL W., of Ashford, bound to Henry Curtis Jr. of Ashford until age 21, which will be on 20 Jun. 1836, to learn the trade of husbandry.

IND. DATE: 02 Apr. 1827   CSL-019M

SMITH, ELIZA, of Middletown, bound to Chansey Whittelsey of Middletown until age 18, which will be in June, 1813, to learn the trade of housewifery.

IND. DATE: 08 Feb. 1808   MHS-001

SMITH, EPHRAIM, ran away from Dr. Eliot Rawson of Middletown. Ephraim is age 26, 5' 7" tall, has black hair, dark eyes, hair grows low on forehead. His teeth are good - one of his lower teeth a little shorter than rest - large dimple in check. Knows farming trade. Reward 40 shillings.

NEWSPAPER DATED: 11 Jul. 1768   CTC-001

SMITH, GABRIEL, brings action against Andrew Sandford for not fulfilling covenant in indenture.

RECORD DATED: 01 Sep. 1659   CSL-012-B

SMITH, HOWARD M., child of Kate M. Smith, bound to Case Lockwood & Brainard Co. of Hartford for term of 3 years, 8 months, 5 days, at which time he will be age 21, to learn the trade of job compositor.

IND. DATE: 05 Jul. 1887   CHS-001

SMITH, JANE, of Middletown, bound to George M. Pike of Middletown until age 18, which will be on 05 Sep. 1851, to learn the trade of housewifery.

IND. DATE: 01 Aug. 1842   MHS-001

SMITH, JARIB, child of Richard Smith, bound to Joseph Adams.

IND. DATE: 13 Mar. 1775   CTH-001

SMITH, MARY, of Farmington, bound to John Ramsay of Farmington until age 18, which will be on 20 Oct. 1836, to learn the trade of housewifery.

IND. DATE: 24 Sep. 1825   CSL-007

SMITH, MARY, of Farmington, bound to Thaddeus L. Thompson of Farmington until age 18, which will be on 20 Oct. 1836, to learn the trade of housewifery.

IND. DATE: 12 Jun. 1827   CSL-007

SMITH, ORRA, daughter of Richard Smith, bound to Samuel Cleaveland.

IND. DATE: 13 Mar. 1775   CTH-001

SMITH, ROBERT ran away from Isaac Sheldon of Hartford. Robert is age 18, 5' 4" tall, has dark hair and dark eyes. Reward $10.

NEWSPAPER DATED: 24 Dec. 1782   CTC-001

SMITH, SAMUEL, of Farmington, child of Elizabeth Smith, bound to his brother Jonathan until age 21.

IND. DATE: 15 Nov. 1676   CSL-042

SMITH, SAMUEL, of Ashford bound to David Allen of Woodstock until age 21 to learn the trade of harness making and farming [Indenture unsigned]

IND. DATE: 1822   CSL-019M

SMITH, SETH, ran away from Peres Comstock of Hartford. Seth is age 19, 5' 6" tall, has long hair and light complextion.

NEWSPAPER DATED: 08 Aug. 1796   CTC-001

SMITH, TIMOTHY, of Farmington, bound to Ezekiel Humphrey of Simsbury until age 15, which will be on 14 Jun. 1799.

IND. DATE: 25 Dec. 1795   CSL-007

SMITH, TRUMAN - NOTE: Mr. Waldo - Mr. Kent called my house and said that Truman Smith, a boy bound to me by the Selectmen of Tolland which he says he should be willing to take the boy and the boy is willing to live there if Selectmen are willing to bind him and I am willing they do so. Signed: Hiram A. Rider.

RECORD DATE: [undated]   CSL-031

SMITH, URSULA, of Farmington, bound to Giles Hooker Cowles of Bristol until age 18, which will be on 20 Nov. 1800, to learn the trade of housewifery.

IND. DATE: 09 Sep. 1795   CSL-007

SMYTHERS, WILLIAM, of Glastonbury, bound to Timothy Goslee of Glastonbury until age 21 to learn the trade of husbandry.

IND. DATE: 04 Feb. 1785   CSL-006

SNOW, ASA, aged 7 in October next, bound to Joseph William Bissell of Lebanon until age 21 to learn the trade of husbandry.

IND. DATE: 14 Apr. 1809   CSL-004

SNOW, CHARLES, age 4 on 14 August last, child of Francis Snow, bound to Bezaleel Fuller of Lebanon until age 21 to learn the trade of tanning and shoemaking.

IND. DATE: 05 Nov. 1810   CSL-004

SNOW, ELIZABETH, bound to Nathan Clark of Lebanon until age 18, which will be on 10 Jul. 1825.

IND. DATE: 17 Oct. 1814   CSL-004

SNOW, ERASTUS, aged about 7 on 1 September last, bound to Julius Bartlett of Lebanon until age 21.

IND. DATE: 12 Jun. 1809   CSL-004

SNOW, HORATIO, of Coventry, bound to Abraham Burnap of Coventry until age 21, which will be on 15 Dec. 1806, to learn the trade of husbandry.

IND. DATE: 16 Jun. 1794   CHS-013

SNOW, MARY, bound to Benjamin B. Fowler until age 18, which will be on 02 Jul.1827.

IND. DATE: 30 Mar. 1815   CSL-004

SNOW, MARY, bound to David Smith of Windham until age 18, which will be on 02 Jul. 1827, to learn the trade of housewifery.

IND. DATE: 26 Aug. 1822   CSL-014

SNOW, MATILDA, of Ashford, bound to Billy Snow of Ashford until age 18. Billy Snow to receive 25 cents per week the first year - thereafter he is to keep her for free.

IND. DATE: 09 Dec. 1817   ATH-001

SNOW, NANCY, of Lebanon, bound to Henry Packer of Colchester until age 18, which will be on 01 Aug. 1844, to learn the trade of housewifery.

IND. DATE: 27 Aug. 1835   CSL-014

SOPER, GEORGE C., born 12 Aug. 1860, child of Charles C. Soper, bound to Case Lockwood and Brainard Co. of Hartford until age 21 to learn the trade of book compositor.

IND. DATE: 05 Mar. 1877   CHS-001

SOUTHURNS, ELIZABETH, of Middletown, bound to George Starr of Middletown until age 18, which will be on 18 Oct. 1808, to learn the trade of housewifery.

IND. DATE: 13 Feb. 1797   MHS-001

SPALDING, RUFUS, ran away from John Norris, Jr. of Tolland. Rufus is age 14, has dark complection pitted from smallpox, talks much but little truth, and delights in talking with old women. Reward 2 cents.

NEWSPAPER DATED: 26 Nov. 1798   CTC-001

SPARKS, JOHN - Petition of John Sparks of Hartford, a minor, by his guardian with evidence showing he was committed to prison in said town on action of trespass for cutting timber on Thomas Matson's land while he was an apprentice to Ezekiel Webster. Praying for relief in equity against Webster who should have saved him from jail. Resolve granting equity to Sparks against Webster passed May, 1752.

RECORD DATED: May 1752   CSL-GA-018

SPENCER, JONATHAN, ran away from Phineas Lovejoy of Suffield. Jonathan is age 17. Reward 2 pence.

NEWSPAPER DATED: 17 Nov. 1794   CTC-001

SQUIRE, BETSEY, of Wethersfield, bound to Chauncey North of Broadalbin, Montgomery County, New York, until age 18, which will be in May 1825, to learn the trade of housewifery.

IND. DATE: 21 Feb. 1820   CSL-005

STANBROUGH, LEWIS - Deposition by Duc Daley, a blacksmith, in regard to the character of his apprentice, Stanbrough.

RECORD DATED: 24 Sep. 1796   CSL-GA-019

STANTON, JOHN, bound to Collins Gorton of Lyme until age 21.

IND. DATE: 07 Jan. 1833   WTH-001

STANTON, SARAH, child of Peter Stanton, bound to Tracy Cleaveland until age 18. Selectmen of Canterbury paid sum to Tracy Cleaveland for taking of indenture.

IND. DATE: 05 Dec. 1785   CTH-001

STEDMAN, CHARLES, ran away from Francis Olmsted of West Hartford. Charles is age 18. Reward $2.

NEWSPAPER DATED: 17 Jun. 1793   CTC-001

STEDMAN, CHARLES, ran away from Francis Olmsted of Hartford. Charles is age 20, 5' 7" tall, has light hair and light complextion. He knows sadler trade. Reward $10.

NEWSPAPER DATED: 31 Aug. 1795   CTC-001

STEDMAN, JUSTUS, JR., ran away from Rogers Sheldon of New Hartford. Justus is age 18, 5' 10" tall, has dark brown hair tied behind, dark eyes, fair skin with ruddy complextion, and is well and strong made. He knows joiner trade.

NEWSPAPER DATED: 01 Jun. 1784   CTC-001

STEDMAN, SIMEON, ran way from Elisha Seymour of Wethersfield. Simeon is age 20, slim, has light complextion, and knows blacksmith trade.

NEWSPAPER DATED: 30 May 1791   CTC-001

STEELE, JAMES, JR., ran away from Henry A. Warner of Hartford. Reward $5.

NEWSPAPER DATED: 27 May 1799   CTC-001

STENNING, WILLIAM, of Wethersfield, child of Phebe Stenning late of Wethersfield, bound to Timothy Francis of Wethersfield until age 21, which shall be in March 1803, to learn the trade of servant. Phebe Stenning is now Phebe Waters of Hartford.

IND. DATE: 03 Mar. 1788   CSL-005

STEVENS, BENJAMIN, ran away from Nathaniel Remington of Suffield. Benjamin is age 19. Reward 1 shilling.

NEWSPAPER DATED: 16 Mar. 1784   CTC-001

STEPHENS, JOSEPH, of New London, bound to Samuel Bradford of New London for term of 6 years, 7 months, at which time he will be age 21, to learn the trade of cordwainer.

IND. DATE: 01 Sep. 1766   CSL-010

STEWART, JOHN, bound to Christopher (Haines) of Lebanon until age 21, which shall of on 01 Apr. 1829.

IND. DATE: 26 Oct. 1812   CSL-004

STIMSON, ABEL, of Tolland, child of Joshua Stimson, bound to Ebenezer Allen of East Windsor until age 21.

IND. DATE: 22 Nov. 1813   CSL-003

STIMSON, SALLY, of Tolland, child of Joshua Stimson, bound to Frank Hatch of Tolland until age 18, which shall be on 19 Aug. 1828, to learn the trade of servant.

IND. DATE: 03 Sep. 1821   CSL-003

STODDARD, ABIGAIL, of New London, age 7, child of James Stoddard dec., bound to Samuel Billings of New London until age 18 to learn the trade of housewifery.

IND. DATE: 06 Apr. 1761   CSL-010

STODDARD, ABIGAIL, of Wethersfield, child of Enoch Stoddard and wife Dinah both dec., bound to Abijah Flagg of Hartford until age 18, which shall be on 10 Feb. 1794, to learn the trade of housewifery.

IND. DATE: 04 Feb. 1788   CSL-005

STODDARD, ANNE, of Wethersfield, child of Enoch Stoddard and Dinah both dec., bound to Phinehas Andrus of Wethersfield until age 18, which shall be on 14 Sep. 1797, to learn the trade of housewifery.

IND. DATE: 04 Feb. 1788   CSL-005

STODDARD, RICHARD, ran away from John Ensign of Salisbury. Richard is age 18, slim, 5' 4" tall, has light hair and light complection. Reward six pence.

NEWSPAPER DATED: 01 Apr. 1793   CTC-001

STODDARD, SAMUEL of Wethersfield, child of Mary Stoddard, bound to William Tryon of Farmington until age 21, which will be on 01 Jan. 1807, to learn the trade of husbandry.

IND. DATE: 19 Feb. 1793   CSL-005

(STORMS), THAMER, of Middletown, child of James (Storms), bound to Benoni Upson of Berlin until age 18, which shall be on 03 Jun. 1806, to learn the trade of housewifery. [Indenture has "Thomas Black" written on back of document].

IND. DATE: 08 Aug. 1796   MHS-001

STONNING, GEORGE ran way from Thomas Mygate of Wethersfield. Reward 2 cents.

NEWSPAPER DATED: 25 Jun. 1798   CTC-001

STONING, WILLIAM, ran away from Timothy Francis of Wethersfield. William is age 17. Reward 2 coppers.

NEWSPAPER DATED: 26 Nov. 1798   CTC-001

STORY, JONATHAN, of Norwich, child of Samuel Story, bound to Curtice Cleaveland of Norwich for term of 1 year, 5 months to learn the trade of shoemaker and tanner.

IND. DATE: 13 Apr. 1740   CSL-017M

STOUGHTON, JONATHAN, of Windsor, child of Thomas Stoughton, bound to Nathan Day of Windsor until age 21 to learn the trades of whitesmith, blacksmith and arithmatick.

IND. DATE: 01 Sep. 1727   WNH-001

STOWE, SARAH, of Middletown, child of Charles Stowe, bound to Harry Shepherd of Chatham until age 18, which will be on 08 Feb. 1846, to learn the trade of housewifery.

IND. DATE: 02 May 1836   MHS-001

STRICKLAND, WILLIAM JAMES, aged 18 years, 6 months, bound to Noyse Billings of New London for term of 2 years, 6 months to learn the trade of seamanship (- going to South Pacific on whaling trip). Indenture made with the approval of Managers of Society of Juvenile Delinquents of New York, New York.

IND. DATE: 24 Mar. 1834   NLH-002

STROEBELL, AUGUSTA, aged 11 years on 25 Mar. 1859, bound to John Clark for term of 6 years, 8 months (at which time she will be age 18), to learn the trade of housewifery. Indenture made with approval of New York Juvenile Asylum.

IND. DATE: 29 Jul. 1859   SHS-001

STRONG, CAROLINE, of Bolton, aged about 9, child of Israel Strong dec. bound to Capt. Roger Barber of Ellington until age 18 to learn the trade of servant.

IND. DATE: 10 Nov. 1830   CSL-011

STRONG, CHESTER, of Bolton, aged about 13, bound to Levi Strong Jr. of Bolton until age 16, which shall be on 05 May 1821, to learn the trade of servant.

IND. DATE: (1818)   CSL-011

STRONG, HOSEA L., of Bolton, bound to Robert Mofett of Hebron until age 21, which shall be on 08 Nov. 1832, to learn the trade of shoemaking.

IND. DATE: 08 Jun. 1831   CSL-011

STUDLEY, OREN, of Tolland, bound to Ashbel Chapman of Tolland until age 21 to learn the trade of husbandry.

IND. DATE: 05 Jul. 1813   CSL-003

SWADALE, ICHABOD, ran away from David Smith of Chatham. Ichabod is age 18, has light, long brown hair, light brown eyes and talks loudly. He is trained as wheelwright. Reward 4 pence.

NEWSPAPER DATED: 07 Jun. 1774   CTC-001

SWATHEL, CHAUNCY, of Middletown, child of ( ) Swathel dec., bound to Levi Parmele of Durham until age 16, which shall be on 27 Jul. 1821, to learn the trade of husbandry.

IND. DATE: 15 Apr. 1816   MHS-001

SWATHEL, CHANCY, of Middletown, child of Jesse Swathel, bound to Timothy Stone of Durham until age 21, which shall be on 27 Jul. 1826, to learn the trade of agriculture.

IND. DATE: 20 Dec. 1819   MHS-001

SWEET, LEYMAN, of Hamilton County, Madison, New York, bound to Lewis Hadsell of Litchfield until age 21 (or age 18 if thought best). Guardian David Ransom states Hadsell is to treat Leyman as his own child.

IND. DATE: 01 Aug. 1863   LHS-003

SWIFT, JABEZ, ran away from Peter Powell of Washington. Jabez is age 19, 6' tall, has long black hair, large, spiteful black eyes, full, well made face, high cheekbones, stout, thick build, and dark complection. Knows carpenter trade. Reward $10.

NEWSPAPER DATED: 14 Jul. 1794   CTC-001

SYMONS, JOHN, ran away from Thomas Cooley of Hartford. John is age 20. Reward one cent.

NEWSPAPER DATED: 09 Jan. 1799   CTC-001

TARDO, ANN, of Wethersfield, bound to Timothy Stanley of Miller Port Township, Rome, Ohio, until age 18, which will be on 08 Jul. 1848 to learn the trade of servant.

IND. DATE: 24 Sep. 1838   CSL-033

TARDO, EDWARD, of Wethersfield, child of Stephen Tardo, bound to Dewet Higgins of Glastonbury until age 16 years and 5 months, which will be on 22 Apr 1852, to learn the trade of servant.

IND. DATE: 02 Apr. 1844   CSL-033

TAYLOR, BENJAMIN, ran away from Alexander McNiel of Litchfield. Benjamin is age 19, 5' 10" tall, has light hair, and knows shoemaker trade.

NEWSPAPER DATED: 02 Jan. 1775   CTC-001

TENNANT, BILL AVERY, ran away from Frederick Pease of Glastonbury. Bill is age 18, middling size, and has light complextion. Reward 2 pence.

NEWSPAPER DATED: 05 Oct. 1795   CTC-001

THOMAS, JOHN, bound to William Champion.

IND. DATE: 12 Mar. 1832   WTH-001

THOMAS, JOSEPH, child of Joseph Thomas formerly of Norwich, bound to Jonathan Bishop.

IND. DATE: 24 Sep. 1830   WTH-001

THOMAS, NOADIAH, of Farmington, age about 15, child of John Thomas, bound to John (Stint) Squire of Farmington until age 21 to learn the trade of farming.

IND. DATE: 20 Jun. 1796   CSL-007

THOMAS, NOADIAH, of Farmington, child of John Thomas, bound to Ashbel Tillotson of Farmington until age 21, which will be on 11 May 1802, to learn the trade of farming.

IND. DATE: 16 Jun. 1797   CSL-007

THOMAS, WILLIAM, of Norwich, aged about 13, child of John Thomas dec., bound to Dudley Woodbridge of Norwich for term of 2 years to learn trade of servant. Indenture made with the consent of his guardian, James Thomas.

IND. DATE: 16 Oct. 1788   STL-003

THOMPSON, HANNAH, of Mansfield, aged between 15 & 16, bound to Charles Harding of Mansfield until age 18, which will be on 10 Jul. 1820, to learn the trade of housewifery.

IND. DATE: 08 Apr. 1818   CSL-001

THOMPSON, JIRAD, of Mansfield bound to Phillip Perkins of Mansfield until age 21, which will be on 31 Jan. 1826, to learn the trade of husbandry.

IND. DATE: 10 May 1812   CSL-001

THOMPSON, ROBERT, ran away from Roswell Griggs of Tolland. Robert is age 18, 5' 8" tall, has short, curly hair and dark complextion. Reward 6 pence.

NEWSPAPER DATED: 14 Mar. 1796   CTC-001

THRALL, JOEL ran away from Thaddeus Taylor of Suffield. Joel is age 19, thick set - middling size.

NEWSPAPER DATED: 21 Aug. 1797   CTC-001

THRALL, WILLIAM, of Windsor, child of Charles Thrall, bound to Francis Griswold of Windsor for term of one year to learn the trade of husbandry.

IND. DATE: 09 Apr. 1773   WNH-002

THRUSHER, JOHN, of Wethersfield, bound to Oliver Richards of Wethersfield until age 16, which will be on 10 Mar. 1831, to learn the trade of husbandry.

IND. DATE: 29 Aug. 1825   CSL-033

TILDEN, SALLY, bound to John Isham Esq. of Colchester until age 18, which will be in February 1840.

IND. DATE: 03 Jan. 1831   CSL-004

TINKER, ISAAC, of New London, aged about 7 or 8, bound to Nathan Tinker of New London until age 21.

IND. DATE: 09 Jan. 1778   CSL-010

TINKER, MARY, bound to Solomon Rogers of New London until age 18 to learn the trade of housewifery.

IND. DATE: 19 Feb. 1779   CSL-010

TONY, BETTY - Claims that while in the service of Joseph Backus, William Bushnell fathered her child and wants support. Court denies support.

RECORD DATED: 08 May 1739   CSL-GA-020

TINKER, SPERRY, of New London bound to Clark Rogers of New London for term of 11 years, ll months, 20 days from 25 Jan. 1775 (at which time he will be age 21) to learn the trade of husbandry.

IND. DATE: 06 Feb. 1775   CSL-010

TINKER, STEPHEN, of New London, child of Jonathan Tinker, bound to Peter Rogers and wife Lucy of New London for term of 10 years, 4 months, and 3 days to learn the trade of mariner.

IND. DATE: 09 Jun. 1751   CSL-010

TOOLY, SARAH, of Saybrook, aged about 8, child of Andrew Tooly, bound to John Barker until age 18 to learn the trade of housewifery.

IND. DATE: 28 Nov. 1778   CSL-043M

TRASK, ARTHUR J., of Hartford, born 31 Mar. 1859, child of Eugene and Melisa Austin, bound to Case Lockwood & Brainard Co. of Hartford for term of 4 years (at which time he will be age 21) to learn the trade of Adams pressman.

IND. DATE: 31 Mar. 1876   CHS-001

TURNER, ELISHA, ran away from Samuel Clark of Winchester. Elisha is age 17, 5' tall and was from New Haven. Reward 2 pence.

NEWSPAPER DATED: 04 Aug. 1788   CTC-001

TRYAL, EUNICE, of Tolland, bound to Gideon Tinkham of Tolland until age 18 to learn woman's work.

IND. DATE: 26 Oct. 1786   CSL-003

TRYAL, EUNICE, of Tolland, bound to John Griggs of Tolland until age 18 to learn the trade of housewifery.

IND. DATE: 01 Jan. 1787   CSL-003

VALLANTINE, JOHN, of Glastonbury, child of John Vallantine, bound to Joseph Goodale of Glastonbury until 07 Aug. 1812 to learn the trade of husbandry.

IND. DATE: 15 Dec. 1801   GHS-001

VALLEY, ELIZABETH, of New London, bound to Joseph Waterhouse and wife Sarah of New London until age 18 to learn the trade of housewifery.

IND. DATE: 03 Aug. 1767   CSL-010

VAUGHAN, GEORGE, aged about 7 on 06 Feb. 1789, bound to Elijah Hyde Jr. until age 17 to learn the trade of husbandry.

IND. DATE: 08 Jun. 1789   CSL-004

VAUGHAN, MARY, aged about 14 of 14 February last, bound to James Clark and Anna Lyman Clark widow of Lebanon until age 18.

IND. DATE: 26 Sep. 1790   CSL-004

WADSWORTH, JEREMIAH, child of Rev. Daniel Wadsworth dec. of Hartford, bound to Matthew Tallcott of Middletown until age 21, which will be on 23 Jul. 1764, to learn the trade of merchandize and keeping merchants. (Indenture made with the approval of his guardian, Mrs. Abigail Wadsworth).

IND. DATE: 24 Sep. 1759   CHS-014

WADSWORTH, THOMAS, of Farmington, bound to Gidor Woodruff of Farmington until age 21, which will be on 19 Oct. 1825, to learn the trade of shoemaker.

IND. DATE: 07 Apr. 1819   CSL-007

WAISTCOAT, STEPHEN, and Matthew Crofut Jr., ran away from Benjamin Knapp and Joseph Benedict of Danbury. Crofut is age 19, 5' 10" tall, has light hair, slim, square face and light complextion. Waistcoat is age 17, 4' tall, has dark hair, dark complextion, round face pitted from small pox. Reward $4 each.

NEWSPAPER DATED: 18 Feb. 1793   CTC-001

WAKE, GRACE, of New London, child of John Wake, bound to Widow Mary Douglass of New London for a term of 17 years, 1 month, at which time she will be age 18, to learn the trade of housewifery.

IND. DATE: 16 Feb. 1761   CSL-010

WALDEN, ABIGAIL, of Tolland, child of Isaac Walden, bound to Capt. Ichabod Hinckley of Tolland until age 18 to learn "woman's work".

IND. DATE: 26 Oct. 1786   CSL-003

WARD, BENJAMIN, ran away from Christopher and Elisha Leffingwell of Norwich. Benjamin is age 19, has short, reddish hair, light complection and middling stature. Reward $4.

NEWSPAPER DATED: 09 Aug. 1774   CTC-001

WARD, CHARLES S., of Middletown, child of Elijah Ward, bound to Thomas Simpson of Middletown until age 21, which shall be on 21 Feb. 1850, to learn the trade of stonecutter. Thomas Simpson is to provide apprentice good set of tools.

IND. DATE: 11 Nov. 1845   MHS-001

WARNER, WILLIAM, of Middletown, child of David Warner, bound to Andrew Bartholemew of Sheffield, Massachusetts until age 14, which shall be on 27 May 1832, to learn the trade of economy & husbandry.

IND. DATE: 15 Sep. 1828   MHS-001

WARREN, WHITING, of Farmington, bound to Jepe Barber of Farmington until age 21, which shall be on 11 Jul. 1826, to learn the trade of shoemaker.

IND. DATE: 04 May 1822   CSL-007

WASHBOURN, DAVID, ran away from Joseph Whitcomb of East Windsor. David is age 16 and 4' 1" tall. Reward 5 shillings.

IND. DATE: 11 Sep. 1781   CTC-001

WATERMAN, YOUNG, of Hartford - Petition by his guardian stated he is about 16 and health is impaired. Waterman was convicted of horse stealing and instead of prison, wants to be bound in service until age 21.

RECORD DATED: 15 Oct. 1817   CSL-GA-021

WATSON, JAMES, aged about 9, bound to Daniel Mackintosh until age 21.

IND. DATE: 05 Apr. 1779   CSL-010

WATSON, NABLEY, of New London, aged about 7, bound to Jabez Beebe of New London until age 18 to learn the trade of housewifery.

IND. DATE: 01 Feb. 1779   CSL-010

WATTLES, JOSEPH, bound to James Pettis of Lebanon until age 17, which shall be on 17 Jul. 1813.

IND. DATE: 17 Sep. 1811   CSL-004

WAY, JACOB, of Farmington, child of Lois Way, bound to Edwin Wadsworth of Farmington until age 21, which shall be on 07 Sep. 1820.

IND. DATE: 25 Jul. 1818   CSL-007

WAY, TRYPHENA, of Wethersfield, child of Betty Way, bound to John Deming and wife Elizabeth of Wethersfield until age 18 to learn the trade of housewifery.

IND. DATE: 04 Oct. 1779   CSL-005

WEBSTER, EBENEZAR, ran away from Stephen Collins of Hartford. Ebenezar is 5' 6" tall. Reward 2 coppers.

NEWSPAPER DATED: 24 Aug. 1795   CTC-001

WEDGE, ZERVIAH, of Norwich, daughter of Joshua Wedge, bound to Daniel Tracy of Norwich until age 18, which shall be on 10 May 1750, to learn the trade of servant.

IND. DATE: 17 Jan. 1736/7   CSL-017M

WEEKS, CHARLOTTE, of Farmington bound to Luke Lewis of Litchfield until age 18, which shall be on 20 Nov. 1837, to learn the trade of housewifery.

IND. DATE: 24 Feb. 1829   CSL-007

WEEKS, HESTER, of New London, bound to Daniel Hurlbut of New London for term of 5 years, 4 months, 7 days, at which time she will be age 18, to learn the trade of housewifery.

IND. DATE: 10 May 1773   CSL-010

WEEKS, JO, of New London, child of Jo Weeks dec., bound to Jonathan Truman of New London for term of 9 years to learn the trade of keeping books.

IND. DATE: 05 Jul. 1762   CSL-010

WELCH, EPHRAIM, ran away from Elisha Barber of Simsbury. Ephraim is age 17, short, has dark brown, short hair, light eyes, and is thick set fellow. Reward $3.

NEWSPAPER DATED: 27 Apr. 1773   CTC-001

WENTWORTH, GIBBENS, ran away from John Watson of Canaan. Gibbens is age 19, has brown hair, brown eyes, and has a considerable scar on one foot. He has scar by joint where great toe joins foot. Reward $5.

IND. DATE: 17 May 1774   CTC-001

WENTWORTH, KATHERIN(E), of Norwich, child of Aaron Wentworth, bound to Hezekiah Huntington of Norwich for term of 7 years, 6 months, 23 days to learn the trade of servant.

IND. DATE: 27 Mar. 1741   CSL-017M

WESCOTT, MARY, of Wethersfield, bound to Amos A. Webster of Wethersfield until age 18, which shall be on 16 Mar. 1828, to learn the trade of housewifery.

IND. DATE: 24 Nov. 1817   CSL-005

WESCOTT, MERCY, of Wethersfield, bound to Oliver Richards of Wethersfield until age 18, which shall be on 16 Mar. 1828, to learn the trade of housewifery.

IND. DATE: 24 Nov. 1817   CSL-005

WEST, HENRY, aged about 12 on 14 Feb. 1808, bound to Israel Williams of Lebanon until age 16 to learn the trade of husbandry.

IND. DATE: 03 Oct. 1808   CSL-004

WETHERLEGG, GEORGE, of New London bound to John Crocker of New London for term of 8 years, 1 month, 18 days, at which time he will be age 21, to learn the trade of mariner.

IND. DATE: 07 Jun. 1773   CSL-010

WETMORE, ANN, child of Thomas Wetmore of Middletown, bound to Edward Fenn of Wallingford for term of 3 years to learn the trade of housewifery.

IND. DATE: 05 Nov. 1770   MHS-001

WETMORE, JOB, child of Thomas Wetmore of Middletown, bound to Isaac Miller of Middletown until 01 Apr. 1772 to learn the trade of husbandry.

IND. DATE: 02 Apr. 1764   MHS-001

WETMORE, MINDWELL, child of Thomas Wetmore of Middletown, bound to Benjamin Wetmore and wife Francis of Waterbury for term of 1 year to learn the trade of housewifery.

IND. DATE: 16 Jan. 1769   MHS-001

WETMORE, PHEBE, child of Thomas Wetmore of Middletown, bound to Simeon Moss and wife Eunice of Wallingford for term of six or seven years, at which time she will be age 18, to learn the trade of housewifery.

IND. DATE: 07 Dec. 1767   MHS-001

WHITE, GEORGE, ran away from Ichabod Wadsworth of East Windsor. George is age 19 and 5' 6" tall. Reward six pence.

NEWSPAPER DATED: 04 Jan. 1774   CTC-001

WHITE, JOHN (alias John Patrick), ran away from Benjamin Henshaw of Middletown. John is age 26, 5' 10" tall, has brown hair and light complection. He also stutters. Reward 20 shillings.

NEWSPAPER DATED: 13 Nov. 1769   CTC-001

WHITTEMORE, HARRIOT, of Bolton, aged about 7 1 July last, bound to Alexander McKinney of Somers until age 18 to learn the trade of servant.

IND. DATE: 13 Dec. 1805   CSL-011

WHITTEMORE, WILLIAM HOWE, of Bolton, aged about 5, bound to Timothy Pearl of Belcher, Hampshire, Massachusetts, until age 21 to learn the trade of husbandry.

IND. DATE: 09 Dec. 1805   CSL-011

WICKHAM, JONATHAN, ran away from Stephen Hutchinson of Hartford. Jonathan is age 21, 5' 6" tall, and stocky. Most likely he went to the sea. Reward $3.

NEWSPAPER DATED: 17 Aug. 1789   CTC-001

WICKWIRE, JONAS, of New London, aged about 11, child of Nathan Wickwire dec., bound to John Wheelar and wife Elizabeth of New London until age 21 to learn the trade of cordwainer.

IND. DATE: 06 Apr. 1761   CSL-010

WILCOX, BENJAMIN, ran away from Elisha Cornish of Simsbury. Benjamin is age 15, has bushy hair, black eyes and brownish complection.

NEWSPAPER DATED: 19 May 1772   CTC-001

WILCOX, CHARLES, of East Hartford, born 09 Jan. 1860, child of Mary Wilcox, bound to Case Lockwood and Brainard Co. of Hartford until age 21 to learn the trade of job compositor.

IND. DATE: 23 Sep. 1878   CHS-001

WILLIAMS, DANIEL, bound to Daniel Chappel until age 21.

IND. DATE: 21 Jan. 1834   WTH-001

WILLIAMS, ELIZABETH, of New London, aged about 11, child of Widow Elizabeth Williams, bound to Ebenezer Weeks and wife Eunice of New London for term of 7 years, at which time she will be age 18, to learn the trade of housewifery.

IND. DATE: 05 Jun. 1769   CSL-010

WILLIAMS, JEREMIAH, of New London, bound to Ebenezer Williams of New London until age 14.

IND. DATE: 09 Jan. 1778   CSL-010

WILLIAMS, JOHN, bound to Capt. Edward Palmer of New London for term of 3 years, 4 months, 3 days to learn the trade of keeping books.

IND. DATE: 05 Jun. 1775   CSL-010

WILLIAMS, JOHN, born in Wolverhampton, Staffordshire, England, bound to Thomas Allen of New London for term of 5 years, 3 months, 5 days (at which time he will be age 21) to learn the trade of sailor or navigation.

IND. DATE: 04 Nov. 1771   CSL-010

WILLIAMS, JOHN, of New London, aged about 14, bound to David Richards Jr. of New London until age 21 to learn the trade of shoemaker and tanner.

IND. DATE: 12 Jan. 1778   CSL-010

WILLIAMS, JOHN, of Mansfield, bound to Dan Swift of Mansfield until age 21, which will be in February 1827, to learn the trade of husbandry.

IND. DATE: 18 Jan. 1820   CSL-001

WILLIAMS, MILLE (Alias), child of Rachel Williams of Wethersfield, bound to Samuel May and wife Mary of Wethersfield until age 18 to learn the trade of housewifery.

IND. DATE: 01 Dec. 1749   WHS-001

WILLIAMS, MOSES, child of Joseph Williams of Norwich, bound to Abner Armstrong of Norwich until the 29th day of January next to learn the trade of joinor.

IND. DATE: 24 May 1745   CSL-017M

WILLIS, CHARLES, of Tolland, child of Madison Willis, bound to Sherman Babcock of Tolland until age 21, which shall be in May 1869, to learn the trade of farming.

IND. DATE: 08 Mar. 1854   CSL-031

WILLIS, GEORGE, orphan of Madison Willis dec. of Tolland, bound to Lucy Main of Tolland until age 21, which shall be on 03 Mar. 1879, to learn the trade of farming.

IND. DATE: 20 Mar. 1866   CSL-031

WILLIS, MARY, orphan of Madison Willis dec. of Tolland, bound to Homer Allen of East Windsor until age 18, which shall be on 15 Mar. 1871, to learn the trade of housewifery.

IND. DATE: 09 May 1868   CSL-031

WIMBRO[W], MARY, child of Anthony Wimbrow of Farmington, bound to Capt. Solomon Cowls of Farmington until age 18 to learn the trade of servant.

IND. DATE: 08 Jan. 1763   STL-002A

WING, AARON, of Glastonbury, binds himself to William Stevens of Glastonbury until age 21, which shall be on 12 Jul. 1801, to learn the trade of house joiner. Indenture made with approval of his guardian, Josiah Hale of Glastonbury.

IND. DATE: 27 Apr. 1798   CSL-006

WING, STEPHEN, of Glastonbury, bound to Josiah Stevens of Glastonbury until age 21, which shall be on 13 Dec. 1803, to learn the trade of house joiner.

IND. DATE: 14 Feb. 1791   CSL-006

WINSLOW, HENRY, of Mansfield, bound to Uriah Hanks of Mansfield until age 14, which shall be on 04 Jan. 1838, to learn the trade of common business.

IND. DATE: 03 Aug. 1826   CSL-001

WITAKER, ABRAHAM, ran away from Harber Howard Wood of Somers. Abraham is age 17, tall, and slim. Reward 6 pence.

NEWSPAPER DATED: 02 Oct. 1781   CTC-001

WOLCOTT, BENJAMIN, ran away from Arodi Higley of East Windsor. Benjamin is age 17. Reward 2 pence.

NEWSPAPER DATED: 07 Sep. 1795   CTC-001

WOLCOTT, DAVID, ran away from Asa Francis of Hartford. David is age 17, rather small and knows blacksmith trade.

NEWSPAPER DATED: 17 Jun. 1793   CTC-001

WOOD, ADDELINE (Alias Ford), of Farmington bound to Jeremiah Cowles of Farmington until age 18, which will be on 15 Mar. 1832, to learn the trade of housewifery.

IND. DATE: 12 Nov. 1818   CSL-007

WOODRUFF, LUTHER, ran away from Thomas Dutton of Watertown. Luther is age 18, has light hair, light complextion. Boy had run away from Sheldon Givens at New Marlborough where Dutton had hired him out.

NEWSPAPER DATED: 15 Sep. 1794   CTC-001

WOODRUFF, PAMELIA, of Farmington, child of Aaron Woodruff, bound to Francis Bacon of Barkhamsted until age 18, which shall be on 20 Jul. 1810, to learn the trade of housewifery.

IND. DATE: 21 May 1800   CSL-007

WOODRUFF, PATTY, of Farmington, child of Aaron Woodruff, bound to M. Case John of Farmington until age 18, which shall be on 22 Dec. 1803, to learn the trade of housewifery.

IND. DATE: 29 Jan. 1802   CSL-007

WOODWORTH, AZEL, of Lebanon, bound to Charles West of Windham to learn the trade of blacksmith. (indenture unsigned and undated)

IND. DATE: (none)   CSL-014

WORNER, EBENEZER, ran away from Isaac Curtis of Harwinton. Ebenezer is age 16 and 5' 5" tall. Reward $2.

NEWSPAPER DATED: 16 Oct. 1769   CTC-001

WRIGHT, ELI, of Wethersfield, bound to Ashbel Wright of Wethersfield until age 16, which shall be on 11 Feb. 1814, to learn the trade of husbandry.

IND. DATE: 19 Mar. 1811   CSL-005

WRIGHT, JAMES, of Wethersfield, bound to James Loomis of Windsor until age 21, which shall be on 15 Jan. 1840, to learn the trade of husbandry.

IND. DATE: 05 Jun. 1832   CSL-033

WRIGHT, JAMES F., bound to Case Lockwood & Brainard Co. of Hartford until age 21, which shall be on 03 Sep. 1893, to learn the trade of job compositor. Indenture made with approval of his guardian J. A. Ross.

IND. DATE: 04 Oct. 1888　　　　　　　　　　　　　　　　CHS-001

WRIGHT, JASON, of Wethersfield bound to Oliver Richards of Wethersfield until age 21, which shall be on 02 Oct. 1841, to learn the trade of husbandry.

IND. DATE: 02 Jan. 1832　　　　　　　　　　　　　　　　CSL-033

WRIGHT, PHILO, orphan living in Mansfield, is bound to Mason Sherman of Ashford until age 21 to learn the trade of husbandry.

IND. DATE: 13 Jun. 1839　　　　　　　　　　　　　　　　CSL-001

WYATT, EBENEZER, of New London, bound to Thomas Leach of Norwich for term of 2 years, 8 months, 5 days to learn the trades of cordwainer and tanner. Indenture made with the approval of his guardian Daniel Coit of New London.

IND. DATE: 21 Apr. 1740　　　　　　　　　　　　　　　　CSL-010

YEOMAN, STEPHEN, ran away from Jacob Robbins of Wethersfield. Stephen is age 19, 5' 8" tall, has short, sandy hair, fair complextion, and scar on thigh.

NEWSPAPER DATED: 17 Jun. 1783　　　　　　　　　　　　CTC-001

YEPPON, CHARLOTTE, aged about 9 on 01 Oct. 1805, bound to Anson Brewster of Bolton until age 18. [Indenture unsigned and only date 1806 appears].

IND. DATE: (1806)　　　　　　　　　　　　　　　　　　　CSL-004

YEPPON, IRA, aged about 5 on 20 Mar. 1805, bound to Gardner Spencer of Lebanon until age 21 to learn the trade of husbandry.

IND. DATE: 24 Mar. 1806   CSL-004

YEPPON, NANCY, age 10 on 19 Mar. 1805, bound to John Bartlett of Lebanon until age 18.

IND. DATE: 24 Mar. 1806   CSL-004

YONGS, ELIPHALET LOOMIS, ran away from Levi Dunham of Glastonbury. Eliphalet is age 16. Reward one penny.

NEWSPAPER DATED: 05 Sep. 1791   CTC-001

YOUNG, MATTHEW - Court Record: Will Williams of Hartford desires to dispose of his servant Young and be released from indenture to teach him trade of cooper.

RECORD DATED: 20 May 1658   CSL-012-G

UNNAMED APPRENTICES

Child of Goodwife Johnson was born in prison and bound to Nathaniell Rescew until age 21.

IND. DATE: 15 May 1651   CSL-012-E

Son of Katherine Liveing of New London, aged about 1 year, 8 months, bound to Joseph Nest and wife Sarah of New London until age 21.

IND. DATE: 02 Jun. 1687   NLT-001

Apprentice ran away from David Brownson of Waterbury. Apprentice is age 24, short, has dark hair, red complextion and heavy dull eyes. Reward $3.

NEWSPAPER DATED: 20 Nov. 1770   CTC-001

Male apprentice ran away from Jeremiah French of Dover, New York. Apprentice is age 25, has large grey eyes, swarthy complextion, and little, right hand finger smaller than normal. Reward $5.

NEWSPAPER DATED: 03 Sep. 1770   CTC-001

Apprentice was bound to Capt. Sherebiah Butt.

IND. DATE: 13 May 1776   CTH-001

Town of Canterbury paid Moses Warren for keeping of Olive Green's child for 3 years and taking indenture of said child.

IND. DATE: 06 Mar. 1780   CTH-001

Apprentice ran away from William May of Wethersfield. Apprentice is age 15, small for age, has light complextion, and is freckled. Reward 4 1/2 d.

NEWSPAPER DATED: 25 Nov. 1793   CTC-001

Dutch servant girl ran away from Lallemant of Middletown. She is age 26, marked from small pox and speak English badly. Reward $4.

NEWSPAPER DATED: 08 Aug. 1796   CTC-001

THEBE - female apprentice - ran away from John Lloyd, Jr. of Hartford. She formerly lived with Mr. Woolsey of Danbury. Reward 13 pence.

NEWSPAPER DATED: 15 Sep. 1778   CTC-001

( ), JENNEY and children (unnamed) bound to Aaron Fish of Groton until debt is paid to learn the trade of servant.

IND. DATE: 15 Jul. 1719   CSL-017M

BLACKS/MULATTOS/INDIANS

ABIGAIL, Negro, bound to Benjamin Tallmadge of Litchfield for a term of one year as a servant. She is then to be returned to Ruth Woodhull of Brookhaven, New York.

IND. DATE: 21 Nov. 1788   LHS-004

APPLETON, Mulatto, of New London bound to John Hewitson of New London for 16 years and 10 days until age 21 to learn the trade of husbandry.

IND. DATE: 09 Apr. 1750   CSL-010

BAILEY, ELI, Negro, of East Haven--Letter to Selectmen of Guilford from Amos Morris. "Sirs you will recollect that some years since the Selectmen of Guilford executed an indenture binding a Negro boy by the name of Eli Bailey to my father Amos Morris...until he arrives at 21...and whereas my father is dead, indenture states heirs have no control of boy." Eli Bailey ran away latter part of September, 1825. Request Selectmen to take charge of the boy.

IND. DATE: 26 Dec. 1825   CHS-002

BARRET, Mulatto, aged about 3 on 28 May last, child of widow Peggy Pomp, bound to Beriah Southworth of Lebanon until age 21 to learn the trade of husbandry.

IND. DATE: 20 Jan. 1794   CSL-004

BETTY, Negro, of New London, bound to Robinson Mumford and wife Sarah of New London for 13 years and 3 months until age 18 to learn the trade of housewifery.

IND. DATE: 20 Sep. 1779   CSL-010

BETTY, Negro, of Farmington aged about 3 on August 1 next, bound to Richard Porter of Farmington until age 21 to learn the trade of housewifery.

IND. DATE: 24 Feb. 1793   CSL-007

BRAND, ROBERT, Mulatto, of New London, bound to Elisha Fox and wife Anne of New London for a term of 10 years, until age 20, to learn the trade of keeping books.

IND. DATE: 10 Jul. 1770   CSL-010

BREWSTER, ERASTUS, Negro, aged about 6 on June 11 last, child of Lemuel Brewster of Lebanon, bound to Isaiah Williams Jr. of Lebanon until age 21 to learn the trade of husbandry.

IND. DATE: 02 Jan. 1809   CSL-004

BUCK, JOHN, Indian, child of Will Buck of Norwich, bound to Howlet Hazzen and wife Zerviah of Norwich to learn the trade of servant for a term of 15 years and 8 months.

IND. DATE: 07 Jan. 1754   CSL-017M

CAESAR, Negro, of New London, aged about one, bound to Robinson Mumford and wife Sarah of New London, for a term of 20 years, to learn the trade of husbandry.

IND. DATE: 20 Sep. 1779   CSL-010

CHARLES, PHEBE (alias Phebe Chew), Mulatto, of Groton, aged about 5 the second day of March last, child of Demmoras Charles (alias Demmoras Chew of Groton) bound to Eliakim Jones of Stonington. Bound until age 18, which will be on 02 Mar. 1812, to learn the trade of housewifery.

IND. DATE: 11 Sep. 1799   NLH-002

COTTENHAM, ABRAHAM, Indian, of Norwich, child of Hannah Cottenham bound to Jacob Hazzen, Jr. of Norwich for term of 18 years to learn the trade of servant.

IND. DATE: 09 May 1752   CSL-017M

COTTENHAM, LYDIA, Indian, of Norwich, aged about 5 years the fifth day of last November. Child of Hannah Cottenham, Indian Single Woman of Norwich, bound to Jacob Hazzen and wife Abigail of Norwich until age 21 to learn the trade of servant.

IND. DATE: 28 Feb. 1750/1   CSL-017M

DAVIS, JAMES, Negro, bound to James M. Broom late of Wilmington, Delaware, for a term of 13 years to learn the trade of house servant. (Indenture drafted in consideration of manumission.

IND. DATE: 01 May 1818   MHS-001

DAVIS, WILLIAM, Negro, of Norwich, bound to John Peabody of Lebanon for a term of 5 years to learn the trade of husbandry.

IND. DATE: 12 May 1826   CSL-045M

DEMMON, DOROTHY, Mulatto, aged about 8 on March 18, 1791, child of Negro man Pomp dec. and white wife, bound to James Fitch Mason of Lebanon until age 18 to learn the trade of housewifery.

IND. DATE: 28 May 1792   CSL-004

DEMMON, JONATHAN, Mulatto, aged about 6 on February 11, 1792, child of Negro man Pomp dec. and white wife of Lebanon. Bound to Samuel Bailey, Jr. of Lebanon until age 21 to learn the trade of husbandry.

IND. DATE: 19 Mar. 1792   CSL-004

DEMING, SOCRATES, "colored boy", of Lebanon bound to William A. Morgan of Lebanon until age 21, which will be on 2 February 1841.

IND. DATE: 31 Aug. 1829   CSL-004

DICK, Negro,--2 February 1801--Town of Hebron paid Elijah House and son for support of Dick, a Negro boy, until he is 21 years old $40.00.

RECORD DATED: 02 Feb. 1801   HBT-001

( ), EBO, Mustee, of Brookhaven, New York, born 26 Mar. 1782, child of Charity (a Mustee), bound to Benjamin Tallmadge of Litchfield for a period of 21 years.

IND. DATE: 07 Apr. 1785   LHS-004

FAIRCHILD, HENRY (sometimes called), of Farmington, Mulatto child of Sume, a Mulatto girl, bound to Romanta Woodruff of Farmington until age 21, which will be on 10 August 1828, to learn the art of husbandry.

IND. DATE: 07 Jun. 1810   CSL-007

FOGG, BETTY, Mulatto, of New London, bound to Thomas Durfey of New London until age 18 to learn the trade of housewifery.

IND. DATE: 22 Apr. 1780   CSL-010

FOGG, MARY, Mulatto, of New London aged about 9, bound to David Richards Jr. of New London until age 18 to learn the trade of housewifery. (age 21 was crossed out).

IND. DATE: 02 Feb. 1778   CSL-010

FULLER, SAMSON, Indian, of Norwich aged about 2 years, child of Genne, Indian woman, bound to Lemuel Bingham of Windham for term of 19 years as a servant.

IND. DATE: 23 Jan. 1746/7   CSL-017M

HANNAH, (Negro) of Wethersfield, daughter of Sampson dec. "free Negro" and Sarah Keeney, bound to Sherman Bordman and wife Sarah until age 18 as a servant.

IND. DATE: 03 May 1763   CSL-005

HANNAH, (Negro), of New London, bound to Elizabeth and Abigail Starr of New London until November 1779, when she will be age 18, to learn trade of housewifery.

IND. DATE: (1769)   CSL-010

JACOB, (Negro) Petition of Moses Bush of Suffield showing that he incurred expense in apprehending a Negro named Jacob who was guilty of stealing cattle from Bush and he agreed to take Jacob into his service to work out costs. Then Jacob immediately deserted petitioner and Bush prays for relief.

RECORD DATED: October 1806   CSL-GA-06

JACOBS, ELISABETH, child of "colored woman" Nancy Porridge of Tolland, bound to Benjamin C. Burdett of Hartford until age 18 which will be on 19 March 1832, to learn trade of servant.

IND. DATE: 19 Mar. 1822   CSL-003

JEFFERY, Negro, born in Colchester, ran away from Stephen Goodwin of Goshen. Jeffery is short, thick, well set fellow. Reward $6.

NEWSPAPER DATED: 07 Jun. 1774   CTC-001

JIM, Negro. A Negro boy belonging to Edward Jessop of Fairfield, guilty of burglary and was bound into service.

IND. DATE: 1817   CSL-GA-07

JOHNSON, JACK (or John), Mulatto, ran away from Elizur Tallcott of Glastonbury. Jack Johnson is 5' tall. Reward $2.

NEWSPAPER DATED: 28 Jan. 1783   CTC-001

JUDE, Mulatto, ran away from Stephen Sedgwick of Hartford. Jude is age 23, 5' 8" tall. Reward $20.

NEWSPAPER DATED: 09 Aug. 1774   CTC-001

JUDE, Negro girl, aged about 7, child of Philu, bound to Jedediah Huntington of Norwich for a term of 11 years, until age 18, to learn the trade of servant. Philu is Negro slave of Dudley Woodbridge of Norwich. Dudley Woodbridge bound Jude to Huntington.

IND. DATE: 08 Dec. 1783   CHS-015

MARK, Negro, bound to Jeremiah Wadsworth of Hartford for life. Mark was sold by Freman Kilborn.

IND. DATE: 18 Feb. 1789   CHS-016

MARK, Negro, aged about 13, bound to Freman Kilborn of Hartford for life as slave. Mark sold by Benjamin Concklin of Hartford.

IND. DATE: 11 Aug. 1788   CHS-014

MARY, "free Negro", aged about 11, bound to Daniel Star and wife Lucy of New London until age 18 to learn the trade of housewifery.

IND. DATE: 06 Jun. 1769   CSL-010

MINT FAGINS/ONEY, Negroes, ran away from Ebenezar Bishop and Ezra Clark of Lisbon. Mint is age 18, 5' 8" tall. Oney is age 20, 5' 8" tall - lost middle finger of left hand. Reward $5.

NEWSPAPER DATED: 14 Jul. 1788   CTC-001

MOSES, Mulatto, ran away from Noah Lane of Killingworth. Moses age 17, thick set, scar on cheek. Reward $2.

NEWSPAPER DATED: 04 Jul. 1791   CTC-001

MURRAY, JOHN, Negro, bound to John Wood of Groton.

IND. DATE: 23 Feb. 1813   WTH-001

NABBY, Negro, of New London, bound to Capt. Robinson Mumford and wife Sarah of New London for term of 16 years, 6 months, until age 18 to learn trade of housewifery.

IND. DATE: 20 Sep. 1779   CSL-010

NANCY, Negro, bound to Benjamin Lyon and wife Sarah of Woodstock for term of 10 years to learn the trade of servant. Nancy was convicted of theft (9 lb. 11 shillings). Must be bound to Lyon to repay debt.

IND. DATE: 22 Mar. 1787   CSL-046

PAGATOON, JOHN, (Indian Man), his wife Sarah and son Sampson bound to Joseph Biglow of Hartford for a term of 5 years for John and Sarah, 19 years for Sampson (until he reaches age 21). John Pagatoon claimed to have the consent of his master Thomas Reaves of Southold on Long Island. Examination of John Pagatoon dated 13/Jul./1723 - Thomas Reaves of Southold claimed said Indians to be runaways. [This case is continued in Hartford County Court Record Book Vol 4, Page 138, dated November 1723. Court denied Reaves claim on Indians.]

IND. DATE: 12 Jul. 1723   CHS-017 & CSL-060

PARSON, PHEBE, "free Indian", bound to Widow Dorothy Bulkley of Wethersfield. Phebe wishing to marry Prince, Negro man belonging to Dorothy, binds herself as servant for the term of the natural life of Prince.

IND. DATE: 10 Jan. 1756   GHS-001

PELEG, Negro, bound to Jeremiah Wadsworth of Hartford term "forever" as slave. Elisha Brewster of Worthington, Massachusetts sold family of Negroes - Peleg, wife Lucy, son Peter and daughter Peggy.

IND. DATE: 23 Aug. 1787   CHS-018

PETERS, EDWARD, Mulatto, ran away from Ezekiel Root of Pittsfield, Massachusetts. Edward has bushy hair, middling stature and lost some teeth. Edward is 35 years old. Reward $8.

NEWSPAPER DATED: 28 Sep. 1773   CTC-001

PETERSON, MARIA, "colored", aged 11 years, 9 months, 10 days, bound to Sylvester Lusk of Enfield for a term of 6 years, 2 months and 20 days to learn the trade of housewifery. Indenture was written with the consent of the Managers of Society for the Reformation of Juvenile Delinquents of New York.

IND. DATE: 14 Apr. 1836   CHS-004

POWENS, MARY, Negro, child of Sophia Powens of Middletown bound to Thomas Macdonough of Middletown until age 18, which will be in February 1836, to learn the trade of housewifery.

IND. DATE: 07 Feb. 1825   MHS-001

REYNOLDS, EMELINE, Negro of Sterling, bound to Abbey Reynolds of Plainfield until age 18 as servant.

IND. DATE: 13 Dec. 1851   CSL-047

( ), ROBIN, Indian of Groton, aged about 9 the 7th of October next, son of Dinah (Indian), is bound to Andrew Lothrop of Norwich until age 21.

IND. DATE: 10 Sep. 1765   ICR-005

SAMPSON, Mulatto, and his squaw and child ran away from Daniel Tyler of Canterbury. Sampson is age 28, 5' 8" tall. Reward $5.

NEWSPAPER DATED: 03 Sep. 1770   CTC-001

SAMUEL, (OR PRINCE), Negro of Middletown, child of Prince, bound to Elijah Hubbard of Middletown until age 21, which will be 08 Nov. 1815, to learn the trade of man servant.

IND. DATE: 28 Dec. 1808   MHS-001

SIMBO, JACOB, Mulatto, ran away from William Miller of Glastonbury. Jacob is tall, slim - age 19. Reward six pence.

NEWSPAPER DATED: 06 Apr. 1789   CTC-001

SKE( ), ROBERT, Indian, of Groton bound to Reuben Brown of Groton for term of 9 years from 15 March last.

IND. DATE: 09 Apr. 1798   ICR-001

SKIPPER, GEORGE, Mulatto, of New London, bound to James Tilley of New London for term of 14 years 9 months, until age 21, to learn the trade of ropemaker.

IND. DATE: 28 Nov. 1766   CSL-010

STORM, CHARLOTTE, Negro, of Middletown, child of James and Sylvia Storm of Middletown, bound to Cyprian Heart of Middletown until age 18, which will be 11 Sep. 1809, to learn the trade of housewifery.

IND. DATE: 09 Aug. 1802   MHS-001

SWAN, ISAAC, "Mulatto or Indian", of Glastonbury aged about 12 the 4th day of September 1791, bound to David Hale of Glastonbury until age 21, to learn the trade of husbandry.

IND. DATE: 27 May 1791   CSL-006

THORN, DOROTHY ANN, "of color", of Farmington bound to Seth Marshall of Farmington until age 18, which will be on 13 Jul. 1831, to learn the trade of servant. ("to live with him at his own risk" written on indenture).

IND. DATE: 04 Dec. 1810   CSL-007

TREAT, TIMOTHY, Mulatto, native of Derby, ran away from George Humphreys of Simsbury. Timothy is 6', has short hair except at neck, speaks slowly, age 23. Reward $10.

NEWSPAPER DATED: 20 Aug. 1798   CTC-001

TUNEY, Negro, ran away from Samuel Gilbert Jr. of Hebron. Tuney age 24 or 25, height 6', very black, talkative. Reward $5.

NEWSPAPER DATED: 15 Jun. 1773   CTC-001

TUNTOGUNO, Indian, of Milford/Saybrook, child of John, alias Chupunk, formerly of Milford now of Saybrook. Bound to Joseph Blaque of Saybrook until age 21.

IND. DATE: 03 Apr. 1727   CHS-019

UNDERWOOD, LUCY, Mulatto, of Stonington, child of York Underwood and wife Mehitabel of Stonington, bound to Nathan Dixson and wife Elizabeth of Westerly, RI until age 18, which will be until 31 Mar. 1816, to learn the trade of servant.

IND. DATE: 04 Jan. 1808   CSL-048

WAKE, STEPHEN, Mulatto, of New London, aged about 5, bound to Capt. (Z)ackeus Wheeler of New London until age 21.

IND. DATE: 02 Feb. 1778   CSL-010

WARRIN, THOMAS, Negro, child of Thomas Warrin of Middletown, bound to Reubin Fowler of Durham until age 21 which will be until 10 May 1813 to learn the trade of husbandry.

IND. DATE: 04 Apr. 1803   MHS-001

WARRUPS, THOMAS, Indian, ran away from Joshua Lovell of Sharon. Thomas is rugged, hearty looking 18 year old. Reward 6 pence.

NEWSPAPER DATED: 18 Feb. 1790   CTC-001

YEPPON, SAMUEL, Negro, aged about 14 on 9 September 1805, bound to Jehiel Williams of Lebanon until age 21, to learn the trade of husbandry.

IND. DATE: 03 Oct. 1808   CSL-004

( ), apprentice boy and Negro servant, ran away from Josiah Griswold of Wethersfield. Boy is age 17, 5' 3", has dark complextion and long black hair. Reward $5.

NEWSPAPER DATED: 27 Oct. 1766   CTC-001

SOURCES

APR ALTON REPOSITORY, SOMERVILLE, MA
APR   -001   Adam Bolin Journal, 1800-1920; Box 7, RG-22

ATH ASHFORD TOWN HALL, ASHFORD, CT
ATH   -001   Selectmens' Records, 1810-1822

**CHS CONNECTICUT HISTORICAL SOCIETY, HARTFORD, CT--
MANUSCRIPT COLLECTION**
CHS   -001   Case Lockwood & Brainard Co.; MS 71342
      -002   Amos Morris to Guilford Selectmen, 26 Dec. 1825
      -003   Windham Justice Court Records; Film 79244
      -004   Lusk, Sylvester *et. al.*; MS 73384
      -005   Owen Family Papers, 1724-1869
      -006   Chapin, Eliphalet, 06 Sep. 1825
      -007   Colton Family MSS; MS 83427
      -008   Davenport, William; MS 71011
      -009   Francis, Justus MS; 13 Dec. 1838
      -010   Preston Selectmen; MS 70251
      -011   Bellamy, Joseph; 1719-1790
      -012   Russell, Richard; MS 74745
      -013   Coventry--Burnap, David, Papers; Box 75
      -014   Wadsworth, Jeremiah, Corrs.
      -015   Huntington, Jedediah, Papers 1743-1818
      -016   Conkling, Benjamin Corrs. 11 Aug. 1788
      -017   Indians; Film 80010, pp. 0425 thru 0427
      -018   Brewster, Elisha, Papers 23 Aug. 1787
      -019   Samson, Occom MSS; Film 79998 Item 1

COT   COLUMBIA TOWN HALL, COLUMBIA, CT
>   COT   -001   Town Records, Pg. 132
>   -002   Town Records, Pg. 6
>   -003   Town Records, pp. 28-30
>   -004   Town Records, pp. 15-16, 26

**CSL   CONNECTICUT STATE LIBRARY, HARTFORD, CT--
ARCHIVES/HISTORY/GENEALOGY**
>   CSL   -001   RG 62, Mansfield; Box 16
>   -002   Probate Record, William Adams; Hartford Dist.
>   -003   RG 62, Tolland; Box 3
>   -004   RG 62, Lebanon Town Financial Records
>   -005   RG 62, Wethersfield; Box 3
>   -006   RG 62, Glastonbury; Box 1
>   -007   RG 62, Farmington; Box 7
>   -008   RG 1, Hartford Particular Court Records
>   -009   Stratford First Congregational Church Records
>   -010   RG 62, New London Town Papers; Box 3
>   -011   RG 62, Bolton; Box 1
>   -012A RG 1, Hartford Main I-Vol. 55/Vol. 2, Pg. 187
>   -012B RG 1, Hartford Main I-Vol. 55/Vol. 2, Pg. 126
>   -012C RG 1, Hartford Vol. I
>   -012D RG 1, Hartford Main I-Vol. 55/Vol. 2, Pg. 183
>   -012E RG 1, Hartford Main I-Vol. 55/Vol. 2, Pg. 15
>   -012F RG 1, Hartford Main I-Vol. 55/Vol. 2, Pg. 5
>   -012G RG 1, Hartford Main I-Vol. 55/Vol. 2, Pg. 54
>   -014   RG 62, Lebanon--Correspondence; Box 6
>   -021   RG 69:29, Zelotes Long; Box 1
>   -031   RG 62, Tolland Selectmens Reports; Box 16
>   -033   RG 62, Wethersfield; Box 7
>   -042   Probate Record Elizabeth Smith-Hartford Dist.
>   -046   RG 3, Windham JP Records; Box 584, Pg. 46
>   -060   RG 1, Hartford Main I/Vol. 4 Court Record Book

**CSL   CONNECTICUT STATE LIBRARY, HARTFORD, CT--
MANUSCRIPT AND ARCHIVES CATALOG**
>   CSL   -013M Barker, Ephraim; Main Vault, 974.62H28B

-015M Mellally, Michael; Main Vault, 974.62N463M
-016M Apprentices, Pomfret; Main Vault, 974.62P77DH
-017M Apprentices, Norwich; Main Vault, 974.62N84IN
-018M Apprentices, New Haven; 974.62N45DB1750
-019M Ashford, Main Vault, 974.62AS36i
-020M Milford, CT, Main Vault, 974.62M59DT
-030M Apprentices, Pomfret; Main Vault, 974.62P77PU
-032M Apprentices, Root, Lewis, 974.62F2275R
-034M Apprentices, Litchfield; Main Vault, 974.62L7Liw
-035M Apprentices, Somers; Main Vault, 974.62SO52C
-036M Leete, William; Guilford; 974.62G94LWR
-037M Indentures, Woodbury; Boyd Coll., 974.62W85B #54
-038M Apprentices, Rixford, Luther, 974.62H355
-039M Winthrop, Robert; 974.6W73 Vol. 3, Pg. 325 A, B
-040M E. Haddam, Bigelow Coll.; 974.62EA746BC, Item 228
-041M Apprentices, Shepard Papers; 920.SH.55
-043M Apprentices, Barker Family; 974.62SA9DB Item 17
-044M Apprentices, Duncan, William; 974.62SH52
-045M Apprentices, Norwich; 974.62N, 84mps Item 2
-047M Apprentices, Sterling CT; 974.62ST4i
-048M Indentures, Avery Family Papers; 920AV35

CSL CONNECTICUT STATE LIBARY, HARTFORD, CT-- GENERAL ASSEMBLY PAPERS

CSL-GA -001 Series I, Court Papers; pp. 380-385
-002 Series II, Priv. Controv.; Film 60-75 117XXV pp. 62-66
-003 Series II, Priv. Controv.; IX, Pg. 40
-004 Series I, Priv. Controv.; IV 124/Roll 104 pp. 101-75
-005 Series II, Misc.; pp. 75-76
-006 Series II, Crimes; V:17, 18
-007 Series II, Crimes; II:131, 132
-008 Series I, Crimes; III:169, 170
-009 Series I, Court Papers; pp. V:118 to 143, 199, 122, 276
-010 Series I, Crimes; III:132A
-011 Series II, Crimes; V:10-12

-012   Series II, Crimes; V:15-16
-013   Series I, Court Papers; pp. 173, 174, 179, 181, 185, and 189
-014   Series II, Crimes; V:24, 25
-015   Series I, Private Controv.; VI: 436-42
-016   Series II, Indus.; II:96
-017   Series I, Crimes; PP. 87 thru 100
-018   Series II, Crimes; XXVI 60-69
-019   Series II, Crimes; V:40
-020   Series I, Crimes; IV:7
-021   Series II, Crimes; V:49, 50

CTC   NEWSPAPER, CONNECTICUT COURANT
CTC   -001   Located both at Connecticut Historical Society and Connecticut State Library

CTH   CANTERBURY TOWN HALL, CANTERBURY, CT
CTH   -001   Selectmens Journal, 1768-85
     -002   Selectmens Account Book; 1819-24

FHS   FAIRFIELD HISTORICAL SOCIETY, FAIRFIELD, CT
FHS   -001   Indentures/Apprentices Collection

FTH   FARMINGTON TOWN HALL, FARMINGTON, CT
FTH   -001   Land Records, Vol. 2; Pg. 315

GFL   GUILFORD FREE LIBRARY, GUILFORD, CT-- MANUSCRIPT COLLECTION
GFL   -001   Indentures/Apprentices Collection

GHS   GLASTONBURY HISTORICAL SOCIETY, GLASTON- BURY, CT--MANUSCRIPT COLLECTION
GHS   -001   Indentures/Apprentices Collection

HBT   HEBRON TOWN HALL, HEBRON, CT--TOWN CLERKS' OFFICE
HBT   -001   Town Records, Town Poor; Vol. I, 1800 -08

-002   Town Records, Town Poor; Vol. III, 1810-31

HRT HARTFORD TOWN HALL, HARTFORD, CT--TOWN CLERKS' OFFICE
HRT   -001   Hartford Town Votes

HTH HARTLAND TOWN HALL, HARTLAND, CT--TOWN CLERKS' OFFICE
HTH   -001   Town Meeting Records, 1761-1833; Vol. 1, Pg. 22

ICR INDIAN AND COLONIAL RESEARCH CENTER, OLD MYSTIC, CT--MANUSCRIPT COLLECTIONS
ICR   -001   Apprentices Collection
        -002   MS 681B835
        -003   MSP 368
        -004   MSB 171888
        -005   MS R552
        -006   MSM 455

KML KENT MEMORIAL LIBRARY, SUFFIELD, CT--MANUSCRIPT COLLECTION
KML   -001   Folder IX, Indentures

LHS LITCHFIELD HISTORICAL SOCIETY, LITCHFIELD, CT--MANUSCRIPT COLLECTION
LHS   -001   Miscellaneous Collection B
        -002   Bolles Collections
        -003   Woodruff Collection, 6310A
        -004   Tallmadge Collection
        -005   Harrison Papers
        -006   Bartlett Collection
        -007   Quincy Collection
        -008   Warren Collection

LTH LEBANON TOWN HALL, LEBANON, CT--TOWN CLERKS' OFFICE
LTH   -001   Town Record Book

MHS MIDDLESEX HISTORICAL SOCIETY, MIDDLETOWN, CT--MANUSCRIPT COLLECTION
MHS -001   Indenture Collection

MNT MANSFIELD TOWN HALL, MANSFIELD, CT--TOWN RECORDS
MNT -001   Town Records, 1806-51; Pg. 226

MTH MIDDLETOWN TOWN HALL, MIDDLETOWN, CT--TOWN CLERKS' OFFICE
MTH -001   Selectmens Memo

NJN NEWSPAPER, NORWICH JOURNAL, NORWICH, NY
NJN -001   Newspaper dated 14 May 1818

NLH NEW LONDON HISTORICAL SOCIETY, NEW LONDON, CT--MANUSCRIPT COLLECTION
NLH -002   Apprentices/Indentures Collection

NLT NEW LONDON TOWN HALL, NEW LONDON, CT--TOWN CLERKS' OFFICE
NLT -001   Land Records; Vol. IV, Pg. 38
       -002   New London Town Hall Town Record Record Book
                 No. 1, Letter E

SHS STAMFORD HISTORICAL SOCIETY, STAMFORD, CT--MANUSCRIPT COLLECTION
SHS -001   Apprentices/Indentures

STL YALE UNIVERSITY LIBRARY, STERLING LIBRARY--NEW HAVEN, CT
STL -001   Chandler Family MSS; 384
       -002   Hooker Family MSS; Box 7
       -002-A Hooker Family MSS; Box 1
       -003   William G. Lane Memorial Collection; Call No. 189

WHS WETHERSFIELD HISTORICAL SOCIETY, WETHERSFIELD, CT--MANUSCRIPT COLLECTION

WHS -001   Wethersfield Indentures/Apprentices

WNH WINDSOR HISTORICAL SOCIETY, WINDSOR, CT-- MANUSCRIPT COLLECTION

WNH -001   Thomas Stoughton MSS
      -002   Miscellaneous Collection

WNT WINDSOR TOWN HALL, WINDSOR, CT--TOWN CLERKS' OFFICE

WNT -001   Windsor Town Book
      -002   Windsor Town Book I 27; Town Acts 1650-75

WTH WATERFORD TOWN HALL, WATERFORD, CT--TOWN CLERKS' OFFICE

WTH -001   Town Book, 1801-34

XRW

XRW -001   Revolutionary War Pension and Bounty Land
            Application Files, M804; Roll 1364

Index

This index does not contain the names of the apprentices as they are extracted in the previous entries. Rather, it contains the names of other interested parties such as apprentice masters, parents, town officials, etc., who appear throughout the entries.

A

Abbot, Abial, 44
Abbot, Ebiel, 33
Abell, Simon, 49
Adams, Alexander Pygan, 5
Adams, Benjamin, 18
Adams, James A., 62
Adams, Jeremiah, 75
Adams, Joseph, 121
Adams, Sarah, 75
Adams, William, 16
Addams, Elizabeth, 1
Addams, William, 1
Akin, Benjamin, 24
Alderman, Wills, 9
Alger, James, 105
Allen, David, 122
Allen, Ebenezar, 20, 127
Allen, Homer, 143
Allen, John, 22
Allen, Miriam, 1
Allen, Samuel Jr., 7
Allen, Thomas, 142
Allen, William H., 2
Allton, Wiliam, 9
Allyn, Solomon, 1
Alvord, Saul, Jr., 109

Ames, David, 105
Anderson, Sawney, 3
Anderson, Sonny, 3
Andrews, Cone, 103
Andrews, David, 4
Andrews, Ezekiel, 73
Andrus, Asa, 3-4, 110
Andrus, Charles, Jr., 85
Andrus, Cloe, 3
Andrus, Frederick, 68, 73
Andrus, Mary, 40
Andrus, Phinehas, 128
Andrus, Thomas, 3-4
Andruss, Almira, 41
Andruss, Phebe, 42
Anthony, Peter, 46
Armstrong, Abner, 143
Armstrong, Amaziah, 4
Aspenwall, James, 109
Atwood, Josiah, 90
Austin, Eugene, 134
Austin, Melisa, 134
Avery, Amos, 43, 99
Avery, Elihu, 5
Avery, Griswold, Jr., 12
Avery, William, 88

B

Bab, Benjamin, 6
Babcock, Sherman, 143
Backus, Abner, 6
Backus, Joseph, 134
Bacon, Francis, 145
Bacon, Pierpont, 90
Bacon, William, 16
Bailey, Lois, 2
Bailey, Noah, 6
Bailey, Roger, 74
Bailey, Samuel, Jr., 152
Bailey, Saxton, 2
Baker, Richard A., 7
Baldwin, Ebenezer, 61
Baldwin, James, 7
Baldwin, Mary, 7
Baldwin, Nathan, 70
Baldwin, Samuel, Jr., 14
Baley, Obediah, 33
Ball, Jonathan, 1
Barber, Capt. Roger, 130
Barber, Elisha, 139
Barber, Jepe, 137
Barber, Michael, 68
Barber, Thomas, 8
Barker, Ephraim, 8
Barker, John, 134
Barnes, Elizur, 81
Barnes, Hartwell, 8
Barns, Eli, 60
Barns, Jonathan, 25
Barret, Oliver, 9
Barstow, Hannah, 10
Barstow, John, Jr., 67
Bartholemew, Andrew, 137
Bartholomew, Mrs. F.G., 22
Bartlett, Chandler, 53
Bartlett, John, 147
Bartlett, Julius, 123
Bates, Moses, 9
Baxter, Elizabeth, 1
Beach, Asa, 59
Beardslee, Hezekiah, 94
Beckley, David, 89
Beckwith, Francis, 10
Beckwith, Joshua, 88
Beckwith, Lydia, 11
Beckwith, Walter, 10
Beckwith, Wilson, 116
Beebe, Amos, 5
Beebe, Daniel, 99
Beebe, Edward, 58
Beebe, Elizabeth, 12

Beebe, Jabez, 137
Beebe, Stephen, 12
Beebee, Jabez, 119
Belden, Mary, 2-3
Belden, Samuel, 87
Bell, Harriet, 14
Bellamy, Rev. Joseph, 104
Bement, Samuel, 14
Bement, William, 35
Benedict, Joseph, 136
Benjamin, Jedidiah, 16
Bennett, Fannie Maria, 15
Bennett, George Augustine, 15
Benton, Benjamin D., 7
Benton, Orrin, 16
Benton, Samuel, 16
Bettes, Priscilla, 16
Bewell, Joseph, 9
Bicknell, Horace, 16
Bidwell, Titus, 66
Bigelow, Isaac D., 57
Biglow, Joseph, 156
Billings, Mary, 13
Billings, Noyse, 129
Billings, Samuel, 127
Billings, Thaddeus, 83
Bingham, Charles, 103
Bingham, Lemuel, 153
Birchard, John, 104
Birchard, Mary, 104
Bird, Josiah, 17
Bishop, Ebenezar, 155
Bishop, Jonthan, 132
Bissel, Ceazar, 1
Bissel, Cloe, 1
Bissell, Joseph William, 123
Blakslee, Jesse, 17
Blanchard, Thomas, 31
Blaque, Joseph, 159
Blin, Hannah, 18
Blin, William, 18
Bliss, Capt. Elias, 108
Boardman, Elijah, 87
Boardman, Jason, 3
Boborn, Edward, 61
Bodwell, Augustus, 111
Bogue, Elisha, 86
Bolin, Alton, 19
Bolin, Dorenda, 97
Bolles, Amos, 32
Bolles, David, 90
Bolles, Ebenezar, 37, 92
Bond, Deacon Jonas, 105

Champion, William, 10, 132
Champlin, John, Jr., 74
Chapel, Jedediah, Jr., 57
Chapill, Jedidiah, 45, 108
Chapill, Joseph, 45
Chapin, Eliphalet, 31
Chapman, Ashbel, 130
Chapman, Jennant, 54
Chapman, Mary, 32
Chapman, Robert W., 118
Chapman, Silas, 18
Chappel, Daniel, 142
Chappel, Jeremiah, 12
Chappel, Joshua, 32
Chappell, Caleb F., 23
Chapple, George, 8
Charles, Demmoras, 151
Chattenton, Daniel, 95
Chester, John, 116
Chester, Mary, 116
Chew, Demmoras, 151
Chew, Phebe, 151
Clap, Nathan, 33
Clark, Abner, 85
Clark, Anna Lyman, 135
Clark, Eliphaz, 34
Clark, Ezra, 155
Clark, James, 135
Clark, John, 129
Clark, Joshua B., 31
Clark, Nathan, 123
Clark, Pat, 120
Clark, Samuel, 134
Clark, Thomas, 40
Clarke, Isaac, 34
Clarke, Moses, 33
Cleaveland, Curtice, 52, 129
Cleaveland, Samuel, 122
Cleaveland, Tracy, 126
Clemmons, William, 34
Clifford, Sylvestor, 30
Coe, Elisabeth, 91
Coe, Elisha, 91
Coe, Joseph, Jr., 89
Coit, Daniel, 146
Coit, John, Jr., 43
Cole, Nathaniel, 98
Collins, Daniel, 76
Collins, John Guilford, 82
Collins, Lyman, 70
Collins, Mary, 69
Collins, Samuel, Jr., 69
Collins, Stephen, 138
Colton, Aaron, 35
Colton, Benjamin, 33

Colton, Cloe, 3
Colton, Horace, 35
Colver, Joshua, 41
Combs, Andrew, 35
Comstock, Benjamin, 81
Comstock, Daniel, 51
Comstock, Peres, 122
Concklin, Benjamin, 155
Cone, Joseph, 35
Cone, Sarah, 35
Cone, William, 6
Confield, Samuel, 106
Congdon, Ruth, 36
Converse, Thomas, 71
Cook, James, Jr., 119
Cook, Phineas, 40
Cook, Sarah, 119
Cooke, William, 36
Cooley, Thomas, 131
Cooper, Samuel, 91
Cooper, Thomas, 8
Copley, Samuel, 37
Copley, William, 37
Corey, David, 37
Cornish, Elisha, 141
Cornwell, William, 37
Cotney, Leonard, 38
Cottenham, Hannah, 152
Cotton, Isaac, 38
Couch, Amos, 38
Covert, Jeremiah, 81
Cowell, William, 5
Cowles, Edbert, 19
Cowles, Elijah, 61, 113
Cowles, Ezekiel Jr., 9, 120
Cowles, Giles Hooker, 123
Cowles, Jeremiah, 144
Cowles, Theodore, 4
Cowls, Capt. Solomon, 143
Coy, Josiah, 2
Crampton, Miles, 113
Crandall, Sarah, 38
Crandel, Elisabeth, 1
Crawford, Charles, 31
Creighton, James W., 39
Crimmen, Mary, 16
Crocker, Elihu, 39
Crocker, Freeman, 39
Crocker, John, 56, 140
Crocker, Truman, 5
Crofut, Matthew, Jr., 136
Crosby, William, 61
Crow, Almira, 41
Culver, Amos, 80
Culver, James, 28

Cunningham, Samuel, 41
Curtice, Reuben, 114
Curtis, Alvin, 42
Curtis, Henry, Jr., 120
Curtis, Isaac, 145
Curtis, Israel, 104
Curtiss, Gabrail, 25
Curtiss, Peter, 27
Curtiss, Prudence, 1

D

D'Oyly, Robert, 42
Daley, Duc, 125
Danforth, Thomas, 115
Daniels, Patrick, 43
Daniels, Pelatiah, 43
Daniels, Silas, 11
Darbes, Ruben, 70
Darrow, Edmond, 44
Darrow, Nicholas, 23, 43
Dart, Joseph, 60
Dart, Samuel, 43-44
Davenport, William, 44
Davis, Hannah, 44
Davis, Phebe, 42
Davis, Samuel, 44
Day, Mary, 18
Day, Nathan, 129
Delphey, Thomas W., 96
Deming, Daniel, 97
Deming, Eliakim, 45
Deming, Elisha, 30
Deming, Elizabeth, 138
Deming, John, 138
Deming, Julius, 75
Deming, William, 73
Dennison, Esther, 46, 78
Dennison, James, 78
Dennison, Samuel, 58
Dension, David, 84
Dewey, Esther, 46
Dewey, John, Jr., 7, 52
Dilling, Desire, 47
Dilling, William, 47
Dillings, Hannah, 47
Dillings, William, 47
Dimmick, Daniel, 63
Dimmick, Eliphalet, 29
Dimock, Shubael, 82
Dixson, Elizabeth, 159
Dixson, Nathan, 159
Dodd, Elisha, 112
Dodd, John, 48

Dodge, Joel, 101
Dodge, Jording, 61
Dodge, Nehemiah, 71
Doolittle, Joseph, 54
Dorchester, Daniel, 48
Dormant, Stephen, 17
Douglas, Robert, 5
Douglass, Hannah, 48
Douglass, Mary, 57, 136
Douglass, Thomas, 48
Downer, Andrew, 49
Downer, Sarah, 49
Downing, Ichabod, 88
Doyle, John, 49
Drake, Levi, 96
Driggs, Joseph, Jr., 81
Duncan, William, 24
Dunham, David, 49
Dunham, Elias, 76
Dunham, Levi, 147
Dunham, Simeon, 74
Durang, Harriet L., 49
Durfey, Thomas, 153
Dutton, Thomas, 145
Dwolf, Simon, 42

E

Eares, William, 50
Easton, John, 18
Eaton, Jessey, 88
Eaton, Luther, 117
Eaton, Simeon, 50
Eaton, Tabatha, 50
Edgerton, Elisha, 48
Edgerton, Nathaniel, 36
Edwards, Betsey, 76
Edwards, Joseph, 11
Ellis, Joseph, 51
Elvin, James, 51
Ensign, (Isaac), 52
Ensign, John, 15, 128
Ensigne, James, 50

F

Fargo, Aaron, 53
Fargo, Ralph, 52
Farnam, Lt. Joseph, 99
Farwell, Isaac, 50
Faxon, Ebenezar, 103
Fenn, Edward, 140
Fielding, William, 13

Filer, Lt. Walter, 8
Finch, Rose Anna, 53
Fish, Aaron, 149
Fish, Elias, 41
Fisher, Christopher, 54, 67
Fisher, Lydia, 54
Fisk, Bezaleel, 14
Fitch, Augustus, 35
Fitch, Benjamin, Jr., 51
Fitch, Capt. James, 93
Fitch, Thomas, 70
Fitch, Warren, 96
Flagg, Abijah, 70, 128
Flanagan, Barnabas, 54
Fletcher, Ebenezer, 115
Flint, Samuel, 100
Floyd, Gilbert, 94
Fobes, Simon, Jr., 118
Folsom, Samuel, 67
Foot, Samuel, 2
Foote, Joel, 102
Forb(e)s, Ruth, 1
Ford, John, 36
Ford, Luther, 88
Fortune, Eunice, 109
Forward, Joseph, 80
Fo(s)dick, Thomas, 55
Foster, Amos, 55
Foster, Cyrus, 4
Foster, Edward, 55
Foster, Mary, 34
Fowler, Benjamin B., 124
Fowler, Reubin, 160
Fox, Anne, 151
Fox, Elisha, 151
Fox, Mary, 56
Francis, Asa, 32, 113, 144
Francis, Charles, 95
Francis, Charles, Jr., 46
Francis, John, 56
Francis, Josiah, 44
Francis, Melisient, 44
Francis, Timothy, 127, 129
Freeman, Azariah, 52
Freeman, Skiff, 1
Freeman, Stephen, 101
French, Jeremiah, 148
French, Joseph, 56
French, William, 57
Fuller, Bezaleel, 83, 123
Fuller, Erastus, 34

G

Galpin, Samuel, 42
Galvin, Patrick, 57
Gardiner, David, 118
Gary, Lucy, 57
Gibbs, Josiah, 58
Gibson, Jacob, 59
Gibson, William H., 59
Gilbert, Samuel, Jr., 159
Gill, Isaac, 59
Gilman, Calvin, 14
Givens, Sheldon, 145
Glasher, Elizabeth, 60
Gleason, Chauncy, 119
Gleason, David H., 40
Gleason, Thomas, 120
Glinn, Peggy, 60
Glover, John, 24
Glover, Sarah, 24
Goff, Alfred, 60
Gomer, Qu(a)sh, 60
Gomer, Voash, 60
Gomer, Vuash, 60
Goodale, Capt. Joseph, 59
Goodale, Joseph, 65, 135
Goodale, Moses, 107
Goodrich, Clarrissa, 73
Goodrich, Hosea, 116
Goodrich, Jemima, 61
Goodrich, William, 70
Goodwin, Richard E., 72
Goodwin, Stephen, 154
Gordon, William, 51
Gorton, Collins, 5, 125
Gorton, John, 81
Gorton, Mary, 81
Gorton, Phebe, 67
Gorton, William, 67
Goslee, Timothy, 123
Graham, Dr. Andrew, 98
Graham, Elizabeth, 61
Graham, John, 76
Graham, Silas, 61
Granger, Thadeus, 95
Grant, Adoniram, 40
Graves, Richard, 78
Green, Alexander, 61
Green, Eunice, 62
Green, Jabez, 86
Green, Olive, 148

Greene, Eunice, 61
Gridley, Henry, 64
Gridley, Mark, 42
Gridley, Samuel, 8
Gridley, Thomas, 26
Griffin, Robert, 116
Griffing, John, 94
Griggs, John, 135
Griggs, Roswell, 133
Griswold, Francis, 133
Griswold, Frederick, 60
Griswold, Joab, 103
Griswold, Josiah, 160
Griswold, Justus, 110
Griswold, Moses, 63
Gro(v)en, Ebenezer, 63

H

Hadsell, Lewis, 131
Hagget, Moses, Jr., 99
(Haines), Christopher, 127
Haines, Daniel, 53
Hale, David, 158
Hale, Elisha, 3
Hale, Elizur, Jr., 102
Hale, Josiah, 144
Hall, Daniel, 34
Hall, Gershom, 99
Hall, Jacob, 6
Hall, John A., 38
Hall, Jonathan, 80
Hall, Thomas, 98
Hamlin, Noah, 64
Hamlin, William, Jr., 92
Hammond, Charity, 64
Hammond, Elijah, 47, 65
Hand, Jonathan, 24
Hanks, Uriah, 144
Harding, Charles, 132
Harding, Mercy, 19
Harris, Hannah, 112
Harris, Hosea, 84
Harris, John, 112
Harris, Joseph, 105
Harris, Richard, 79
Harriss, Joseph, 42
Ha(rr)y, James, 66
Hart, John, 109
Hart, Lucinda, 66, 108
Hart, Norman, 75
Hart, Selah, 66
Haskel, Elijah, 50
Hatch, Frank, 127

Hatch, Jonathan, 33
Hawley, Elijah, 66
Hawley, Levi, 70
Haws, Eli, 33
Hayden, Nathaniel, 99
Hayden, Nathaniel, Jr., 90
Hayes, Joseph, 66
Haynes, Elias, P., 108
Hazzen, Abigail, 152
Hazzen, Howlet, 151
Hazzen, Jacob, Jr., 152
Hazzen, Zerviah, 151
Heacock, Joseph, 1
Heacock, Samuel, 1
Heart, Cyprian, 158
Heel, Samuel, 90
Hempsted, John, 106
Henshaw, Benjamin, 53, 62, 141
Herrick, Rufus, 67
Hewett, John, 52
Hewett, Ruth, 52
Hewitson, John, 150
Higbe, Samuel, 67
Higbee, John, 13
Higbee, Sarah, 13
Higby, Samuel, 67
Higgins, Dewet, 131
Higgins, Prince, 10
Higley, Arodi, 144
Hill, Charles, 13
Hillhouse, Wm., 12
Hills, Abijah, 68
Hills, John D., 4
Hinckley, Capt. Ichabod, 45, 136
Hinckley, Ichabod, 110
Hinsdale, Elijah, 118
Hinsdale, Capt. Wolcott, 19
Hinson, Sarah, 68
Hoadley, Silas, 113
Hodge, John, 69
Holester, Appleton, 57
Hollister, Bethiah, 76
Hollister, John, 54, 65
Hollister, Joseph, 76
Holmes, David, 74
Holt, William, 43
Hopkins, Joseph, 108
Horner, Thomas, 71
Horton, John, 30
Hosmer, Stephen, 41
House, Elijah, 153
Hovey, Aaron, 108
How, John, 90
Howe, Ephraim, 71
Howe, John, 71

Y